Bethany

Adventures Of The
Mighty Mustard Seed

By

Bernard Kearse

PRESS

Maps drawn by Mary Clare Kearse
Cover Design by D. Garrett Nantz

In memory of my father, Bernard V. Kearse, Jr.,
whose sense of humor I fondly remember,
and Reverend Douglas Verdin who set the spark
for this book and encouraged my efforts.

TABLE OF CONTENTS

CHARTS AND MAPS

Chapter 1
Straying From the Path

All she wanted was a dog – a nothing-special-about-it dog. A mutt would do just fine. Straight from the pound, she didn't care. Bethany wanted one that badly, and she wanted one now! Was that too much to ask? She'd be off to college in just six short years, and, well, her youth was slipping away fast. She hadn't much time left. That's the way she saw it. But it wasn't going to happen: not now, not ever! Her parents had promised her a dog when they moved to Salem City a year ago, but then changed their mind. They gave her a bunch of feeble excuses from time to time. But she didn't buy them, not a single one. She knew the real reason for her dogless home, and, boy, was it pathetic! The family secret – no one would discuss the real problem, but everyone knew. It made her mad sometimes, and often very sad.

But she could daydream about it, which is what she was doing when Mrs. Fanneyspankel announced in her squeaky mouse-like voice, "Bethany, will you please pay attention to your Sunday school lesson? Child, you need to get more sleep at night. You're forever drifting off in our class."

Bethany shook her head to wake herself up. "What, Mrs. Fanneyspankel? I was ... just thinking about things," Bethany said trying to appease her teacher, although today she didn't much care what her teacher thought. She was sick of trying to be nice when she was bored, mad and sad, all at the same time: It was Mrs. Fanneyspankel's fault – no, no, it was her parents' fault! They needed to deal with this "dog" problem that was consuming their child! This isn't the way a sixth-grader should be forced to live, she was thinking when her teacher continued.

"Bethany, maybe you can lead us in our next song – Beulah Land. That should wake you up!"

"Oh, great, like I really want to lead the singing," Bethany said under her breath just softly enough not to be heard.

"Well, what about it, Bethany? Lead us," Mrs. Fanneyspankel continued.

Bethany turned to her and said with a forced smile, "All right, let me just clear my throat." Below the surface, Bethany was ready to explode, but had been taught by her mother to act nice until it hurt. Finally, Bethany began the song as she bellowed out in her strongest, full-lung-power, nothing-held-back, church-going voice, "I'm liv-ing on the moun-tain, underneath a cloudless sky, I'm drink-ing at the foun-tain that never shall run dry; O yes! I'm feast-ing on the man-na from a bountiful supply, For I am dwell-ing in Beeeu-laah Land!" Wow, that felt good, Bethany had to admit to herself; singing could be a great stress reliever. And when she was in a good mood, she would readily admit that singing was the best part of Sunday school without question, except for kicking Bobby Barton's chair and watching his face get beet red: OK, just radish red, but her mom always said beet red. (Once her mom had referred to a neighbor who had her totally flabbergasted as "that old cabbage face." Bethany had never quite figured that one out.)

Singing about the cloudless sky of Beulah Land in Sunday school was good on a day like today. It had rained daily for the past two weeks, and while on this April morning the sun was finally shining, Salem City certainly wasn't Beulah Land, Bethany thought. In fact, she was beginning to wonder whether Salem City was really part of the "sunny South." She might as well be back in Connecticut, where she had previously lived. She liked her new home but, well, Connecticut was where most of her friends were, and she missed them a lot. Moving was hard for a twelve-year-old.

Riding in the car with her parents, her teenage brother, Stopher, and her younger sister, Genny, Bethany reflected on the song she had just sung in Sunday school. "Dad, where is Beulah Land?" she blurted out during a rare moment of silence in the Clarke family's big sedan. (Mr. Clarke liked to take long automobile trips. He once said that packing people in a car like a can of sardines and hitting the open road was the glue that held the American family together.)

"Beulah Land? Isn't that the new biblical theme park that opened near here last month?" Dad responded. Dad was an incorrigible kidder. "Yeah, that Noah's Ark ride there is a real killer! Two children almost drowned on it last week."

"Be real, Dad!" Bethany said. "I'm serious."

"I was confused. Forgive me. It's that new supermarket going up on Charity Road. Has lots of fresh dairy products," Dad commented with a smile.

"Stop kidding her, honey," Mrs. Clarke interjected. Knowing her husband was on a "roll" and would not easily be diverted, she commented, "It's symbolic for the Holy Land, I think, dear."

"What part of the Holy Land?" Bethany inquired, feeling she was making progress.

"Bob, help me out here," Mrs. Clarke said to her husband.

Happy to be back in the conversation, Bob replied, "Oh yes, Beulah Land includes most of Israel, parts of Palestine, Judea, Samaria and the northwest corner of the Transjordan, or is it the southwest?" Mr. Clarke had a knack of saying just enough to sound almost authoritative, but not quite. Creative chaos was his game. Throw out an idea or a fact or two and let the conversation follow. Bethany had experienced many such discussions with her dad, and she had developed methods to ferret out some semblance of the truth.

"OK Dad," she said. "What's the difference between Palestine, Judea and all those other places you just mentioned?"

Stopher decided to get into the act. "Dad, you're just blowing smoke!"

Mr. Clarke sensed a contest. He knew that he had to be careful here. The family was beginning to gang up on him. He was good at back-pedaling – lots of practice. "It's quite complicated, but if I had a map, I could easily show you. It all relates back to the twelve tribes of Israel. I'll get a map out when we get home," Mr. Clarke said, knowing that this ploy bought him time and that the kids would become involved in other activities and forget all about their inquiry.

"Is Beulah Land in the Bible?" asked six-year-old Genny, remembering her sister's earlier question.

Mr. Clarke thought for a moment, realizing he had overstimulated the conversation on this subject and had to have a major curve ball to land a strike-out. "Don't you kids learn anything in Sunday school? You know, the Clarkes are supposed to know the Bible. Our great-great grandfather used to carry one in his saddlebag. I'm going to make sure that each of your knapsacks for school has one. And another thing, if you're not getting a proper religious education, don't blame me. If it wasn't for your mother's bad knee, we'd be Episcopalians!"

"Bob, stop that!" Mrs. Clarke said. "There's absolutely nothing wrong with my knees."

"Daddy, why do Episcopalians go to church on Saturday?" Bethany asked.

Mr. Clarke sighed with great relief. His ploy had worked. "No. No! It's the Seventh-day Adventists that go to church on Saturday!" Dad happily retorted. "Ask your mother why. She used to date an Adventist, you know. Didn't you Nancy, dear?"

Mrs. Clarke had had enough. "I dated lots of boys, but that doesn't mean we discussed in detail their religious beliefs!" she snipped.

Bethany could tell her mom was ready to call Dad a "cabbage face" when, suddenly, a sound like a small explosion occurred just inside the engine of the car and startled Mr. Clarke so badly that he swerved to one side. His face grimacing, Mr. Clarke gripped the steering wheel tightly as the automobile chugged to a halt by the side of the road.

"Is everyone OK?" Mrs. Clarke then caught her breath before looking around to the back seat to find her three "angels" buckled in safely. Bethany, Stopher and Genny nodded. With a sigh of relief, Mr. Clarke got out of the automobile to check under the hood. Stopher, not wanting to be left out of the action, bravely marched alongside his dad to the front of the car. Bethany slid back into her seat opting to let the guys handle this one.

"Dad, this doesn't look good," Stopher examined the steam rising from the aging "Clarke-mobile."

"Stand back son," Mr. Clarke said while opening the hood to reveal a massive cloud of white smoke.

Sticking her head out the window, Genny attempted to

get her dad's attention. "Daddy, I gotta go to the bathroom."

Mr. Clarke could feel the pressure to take charge of the situation. He observed the still-smoking engine meticulously. Although he knew his knowledge of cars was pitiful at best, he didn't want the family to know that he didn't know what to do. They were in an unpopulated stretch of road approximately five miles from Uncle Lot's home. (Lot was Mrs. Clarke's much older half brother who they visited for Sunday dinner every other week.) Mr. Clarke, viewing the engine said, "Unfortunately, it looks like the carburetor is hyperventilating to the manifold and this is transfixing the vector shield."

Stopher, looking over his dad's shoulder said, "Dad, are you sure it's not just a busted water hose? I mean, you've got some water coming out from over there by the radiator."

Mr. Clarke, not to be outdone, patted Stopher on the head, "I can understand how to the untrained eye it could look that way son, but I'm pretty sure that it's much more complicated than that." "Well," Mr. Clarke continued, "I believe we've got to call the towing company on this one." As he whipped out his mobile phone to make the needed call and the rest of his family piled out of the vehicle, a late model car rounded the bend ahead and pulled over as the driver inside said, "Need help?" For a moment, Mr. Clarke almost told the old man "no," but then realizing that his mobile phone was not working properly, he said "Sure. Thanks. Know anything about engines?"

As the old man got out of his car, Bethany noticed a small Bible in his shirt pocket and a set of keys hanging from his belt. His clothes were soiled in spots, and she could tell he was the "handy man" type. She wondered if he was a custodian for the school they had passed just a few miles back.

Viewing under the hood, the old man got a fix on the

problem, saying, "I think I can get to the bottom of this. Let me grab some tools. Got just about anything you can think of in here," he said pointing to the trunk of his car. "Sometimes people don't think to ask," he continued as he collected some tools and tape and went over to the engine. After about five minutes, he said "I'm pretty sure I found the problem," and then returned to his trunk to collect additional tools he needed to complete his task. As he worked, he could overhear the family's conversation. It revolved around Uncle Lot. For the past year, their family had Sunday dinner with him after church – one week his house, next week theirs. He lived in a stately mansion that was surrounded by a small lake. The house topped a lovely forty-acre tract overlooking a delightful meandering stream. Grazing about the property was a large herd of cows. Lot had recently retired early due to the small fortune he had amassed as a shrewd businessman in the cookie industry.

Bethany's uncle had many pearls of wisdom. He liked to mention his name in his brief sayings. A few of his favorites were: "There's a *lot* of money in cookie dough," or "if you *kneed* the dough, *lots* of *dough* will follow" or "*lots* more where that came from." Bethany didn't always understand what her uncle meant, but she heard these "Loterisms" so often that she couldn't help but remember them, even if she found them annoying. The one most revolting to her was, "You know, if I didn't talk a *lot*, I might forget my name. Boy, I've got a lot to remember." *Lot* thought that one was particularly humorous. This repetitive dinner ritual was often tiresome for Bethany and her siblings.

As the family stood along the side of the road, Bethany asked, "Daddy, can we keep it short today? I mean, let's not hang around after lunch. Uncle Lot can drive me crazy with all his talking and all that business stuff. Sometimes I just get sick of it!"

"He does talk a lot, doesn't he? But if he didn't, he

might forget his name!" Dad teased, trying to get Bethany irritated.

Mrs. Clarke interrupted, "Bob, you're impossible. Don't rib her like that." After a moment of silence, Mrs. Clarke spoke again. "Now, Bethany, your uncle can be trying sometimes, and I must admit I almost never agree with him on anything political. But he is family, and it's important that family stay close. You know, we're really all he has. He doesn't have many friends. And I know he loves you kids. But for some reason, he just doesn't know how to show his affection." (The old man continued to work on the engine as he overheard the conversation.)

"Mom," Bethany added, "I know he is smart on business things. But he's so wrapped up in what he's saying that he hardly knows who we are. And I'm not certain he cares. I think I know why he never married: He couldn't take time out to learn his girlfriend's name!"

"Bethany Anna Clarke," Mrs. Clarke began, "you watch your mouth, young lady. You are going overboard and don't know what you're talking about."

"I know enough to know that old codger is the reason that I can't get a dog! And it's not fair! Just because he has some little allergy problem, I have to suffer!"

"Yeah," Stopher joined in, "why do we have to have a dog-hair-free house just so he can come over to dinner every other week? That's about the only time he ever comes to see us anyway. Why can't we just go out to eat like normal people? And, at his house, I feel like we're in a museum or something."

"Children, that's enough. We've had this discussion a hundred times before. We're already thirty minutes late for dinner and this is going nowhere. Now straighten out and let's get back in this car as soon as it's up and running. And when we get to your uncle's house, please just go inside and behave yourselves. And remember your manners at the dinner table."

Shortly thereafter the old man announced, "It's ready to go. Nothin' major, just needed a bit of work here and there."

Mr. Clarke told the old man how much he appreciated his help and attempted to give him some money, but he refused to take it. "No thanks. Where I'm from, I don't really need it. Thanks just the same." Getting into his automobile to leave, he motioned to Bethany to come over to his car. While the other family members were distracted by Stopher and Genny's argument on who was going to sit by the window, the old man looked directly at Bethany and smiling said, "We all have much to give and much to learn from each other. Share the joy!" Bethany stood silently as the old man started his car and pulled away.

Back on the road, Mr. Clarke said as he continued the drive to Uncle Lot's home, "You know, that was a nice guy who helped us back there. I didn't even get his name. I guess we got tied up in our conversation and forgot to ask. He would be a good person to get to know." Bethany nodded in agreement, continuing to reflect on what the old man had said to her a few moments before.

*   *   *   *   *   *   *

It was a typical lunch with Uncle Lot. He was his usual pontificating self – telling more and more stories of successful business strategies, while the other family members attempted to get a word in edgewise. Bethany tried to engage her uncle in a conversation on the benefits that animals can bring to a family.

"Uncle Lot," Bethany started, "you ought to think about getting a pet."

"A pet? You mean like a dog or something?" he responded. Lot was a large man with mammoth hands, hands too large even for his hefty body. And his gruff, booming voice could be intimidating to a young person.

"Yes."

"Why would I do that?"

"It would probably do you some good, being all alone here in this big house," she observed.

"But I don't need a dog. I've got one of the finest security systems money can buy, Bethany. Look around this house. I've got three cameras in this room alone," he said as his enormous hands pointed like pistols to each. "And the rest of the house is covered with them too. Over seventy cameras all together, if you count the ones covering the outside grounds. And my alarm system is so loud that it would wake up the dead! You know, this house is more secure than any castle in Europe, with a moat to boot. You know, it cost me a bundle to create that little lake that surrounds this fort, but when I pull up that bridge at night, I sleep like a baby. And I just dare anyone to swim across that moat with my alligetters guarding the house. Just got those beauties last week!"

Everyone at the table seemed surprised at this statement. Finally, Stopher asked, "Uncle Lot, what's an alli-getter?"

"Son, they're alligators that have the temperament of crocodiles and have been specially bred to live in cold water environments. Took ten years to develop, but I think there's probably a big market for these critters. I understand that they can live outside as far north as New Jersey. I don't know; this could be a good business to invest in. I got to hand it to that Mr. Frugly in Florida. He has really bred some nasty predators." Then Lot paused before continuing, "No, Bethany, I don't need a dog. I got all the security I want. Iron clad. Like Fort Knox." At that moment Uncle Lot pushed himself away from the table, and placed his hands behind his head, leaning back in his chair to enjoy the moment of satisfaction with a house well built to withstand any imaginable type of "intruders" that might lurk outside.

Bethany sat quietly, fuming as Lot had gone on and on

about his fortress and not understanding what she meant. "I'm not talking about... about your security, Uncle Lot. I'm talking about a dog to greet you when you get home and to make you happy! Don't you want something alive to take care of – something cute and cuddly?"

"Bethany," Lot said, as he thought for a moment, "dogs are time-consuming and messy, shedding their fur all the time. You know, if I can't raise them to sell, I really don't see the need. Plus, they could give me a 'lot' of trouble with my allergies. Naw, dogs aren't worth the hassle," he said shaking his head as he spoke. "Let's look at it from the practical side."

Bethany's eyes focused on her uncle as her anger continued to build. Her head began to swim as she thought her body would burst, given the rage bubbling up inside her. Finally, she could hold it in no longer, as she yelled, "Forget practical! I hate practical! And I hate you Uncle Lot! You are as cold-blooded as your stupid alligetters!!" Bethany then banged both fists on the dining room table, toppling her iced tea glass, and stood up abruptly, knocking over her chair. She then began to bawl as she exited the room and ran to the front door of the house.

The rest of the Clarke family was frozen in shock. Bethany had never acted so badly before. In a moment, the silence was broken by Genny who began to cry as she ran over to Mrs. Clarke for comfort.

Lot was taken aback for a moment. Finally he said, "Nancy, she shouldn't talk that way to her uncle! And what did I say? I mean, what's she talking about?"

"Lot, I'm sorry. I don't know what to say. What she said to you was totally unacceptable. Bethany will be punished, of course. There must be something wrong. I'm really sorry."

The ride home was a quiet one. Before Bethany got out of the car, Mr. Clarke told her to go to her room and wait there while he and Nancy decided on her punishment.

Bethany complied, but when her parents came to her room to discuss the matter, things went badly, very badly. She couldn't calm down, and both she and her parents had "words" that were extremely unpleasant. Finally, her parents told here that she was "grounded" for a week, and the only two things she could do outside the house were practice her basketball and go to her friend Allison's house to borrow her science textbook, since Bethany had mistakenly left hers at school on Friday.

As Mr. Clarke sat down to read his newspaper, Stopher followed the children's Sunday ritual of working on homework or reading for an hour after lunch. Bethany was too upset to do either. She paced around in her room and decided she could take no more. She was going to run away! "I'm outta here!" she mumbled to herself. This would show her parents and Uncle Lot! She would return to Connecticut and live with one of her friends who would definitely let her have a dog. As she began to pack her suitcase with the bare necessities, she calmed down a bit and thought about how she could make this long trip. While she may have had enough money to buy a bus or train ticket, she realized that planning such an escape would not be easy. She would have to think it through step by step. "No rush," Bethany thought as she pushed her partially packed suitcase under her bed. "I must act natural so that Mom and Dad won't suspect a thing. Tonight, I'll plan it all out and leave tomorrow after school." She felt better. She was in control – or so she thought.

Bethany finally decided to get some exercise by practicing her basketball so she put on her faded jeans, a pair of sneakers and her favorite violet-colored shirt that her mom had worn years ago. While dressing, Bethany, for some reason, began to think about what the old man on the road had said to her; it rattled around in her brain as she tried to understand it. After tying her last shoelace, she went downstairs and out the back door. Once outside,

Bethany worked hard for over forty minutes on her basketball moves as part of her daily ritual at the backyard goal her dad had installed. She was good and getting better every day. Her shirt was a bit worn, perfect for tramping through the woods, which was where she was heading after her practice. Her new friend, Allison, lived in the next subdivision that was separated from hers by a fifty-acre park. While heavily wooded, the park had a narrow, winding path – connecting the two subdivisions – that easily could be followed until mid-summer, when the underbrush became quite thick. Since it was still early spring, Bethany decided to take the cut-through to Allison's house.

The clouds cleared and the sun was shining brightly by mid-afternoon. And while this had been one of the wettest on record, spring was generally magnificent in Salem City. Wild dogwoods engulfed the park with their fresh blossoms, looking for all the world as though tens of thousands of white butterflies had been frozen in mid-flight. Bethany went down to the path, at first unappreciative of the sunshine that was greeting her. But a few minutes among the dogwood blooms made Bethany almost forget her homesickness for her friends in Connecticut. The path seemed mystical with its beauty. Nearly halfway into the park was a small stream, and on the other side was an old wisteria vine with its enchanting blooms of purple growing up a massive water oak.

Bethany decided that she must take some of these grape-like blossoms to Allison. There was one slight problem with retrieving this prize. The streambed and the path were at the bottom of a steep gorge that she would have to climb to reach the oak tree housing the wisteria. While her parents had always told her never to stray from the path, she felt that this was a prize worth the risk. Besides, she would be able to see it from the top of the ridge, so maintaining visual contact with the path could be argued to be within the "no straying" rule. She hesitated for a moment, thinking through her argument. The purpose of the rule was to keep her from becoming lost. Therefore, she concluded, in her precocious mind, staying within eyesight of the path was technically not straying. "Dad would like such a logical conclusion," she whispered to herself. "Besides, who could get lost in a fifty-acre park?"

The slope she climbed was slippery, but Bethany crawled up, a toehold here, a toehold there. She grabbed the bases of small bushes to help with her balance. Twice she slipped but caught herself on outreaching tree branches after sliding back a couple of feet. Finally, she reached the top of the ridge where the oak stood majestically. This was an area she had never explored before. The ridge itself was very narrow, probably no more than seven feet at its widest point. And the view of the other side was splendid. Many more dogwoods dotted the sloping terrain, and, at the bottom, a small pond framed by lily pads was alive with waterfowl. At the far end of the pond stood a magnificent cherry bark oak nearly one hundred feet tall. Bethany gasped. It was all too picturesque for words. She wondered whether she should dare tell her parents that she had discovered this "garden of Eden."

Bethany again focused on her objective – the wisteria blossoms – as fragrant as any flower on earth, she thought. The best blooms were at about seven feet, slightly out of her reach. She looked about, surveying the territory for an instrument to achieve her mission. On the pond side of the ridge, she spotted a short, fat log that was approximately a foot thick. It would be heavy but, if she could roll it over to the tree, she could probably reach the blossoms of her choice. Moving down the ridge so that she was below the log, she began to slowly push it up the embankment. She was within two feet from the top when her foot caught on a dead tree branch on the ground. Suddenly, her hands flew into the air as she frantically tried to grab a limb to steady her balance. Failing to grasp one, she fell to her side and began to cartwheel down the hill toward the pond below. Rapidly tumbling down the slope, she began to scream, realizing she was likely to collide with one of the sharp boulders beneath her. She avoided one, two, three rocks and continued her descent. But the rugged edge of a fourth boulder whacked her head, and her body came to rest – motionless at the bottom of the hill. All became dark and silent.

Chapter 2
Zap! A Brilliant Light

It appeared to be nearly dusk when Bethany awoke. Dazed, she saw what appeared to be a flash of brilliant light followed by a spiral of translucent blue butterflies just a few feet away. Her mind cleared, and she moved her head slightly to one side blinking her eyes. As her vision returned, she suddenly realized that she was staring directly into the face of a man she had never seen before! She jumped up quickly and ran away from the man, knocking the tree branches away from her face as she ran recklessly through the woods. Finally, she approached a clearing ahead and believing she was out of danger slowed down only slightly. Entering the clearing, the man suddenly appeared directly ahead of her! Letting out a shriek, Bethany spun around and began running across the corner of the field, hoping to escape. Her heart pounding hard, she approached another corner of the woods when once again the strange man appeared ahead of her in the distance. Confused, she once again turned around and ran back toward the clearing. Reaching the middle of the field, Bethany tried to catch her breath as she looked back to see if the man was anywhere to be found. Seeing no one, she was amazed when she heard a voice.

"Young lady, why do you run? You can't escape me."

Bethany whirled around but still saw no one. Suddenly she felt a slight tap on her shoulder. Turning, she saw him once again in front of her and decided that she must confront him directly.

"Who ... who are you?" she asked, with a tremble in her voice. Studying his face, she guessed his age to be around the late twenties or early thirties. He had a kind smile, but something immediately told her that he was strange, different. "Why are you wearing a skiing outfit?" she blurted out. (Yes, it was a snowsuit – quite sharp, really – the kind she imagined a movie star vacationing in Aspen or Vail would wear.)

"I have this skiing attire on because it is what I wear when I ski, which is exactly what I was doing when your ... your situation," he paused, "...presented itself."

Bethany was perplexed. Either she was dreaming or she was talking with a complete idiot! She rubbed her eyes, but the strange man still appeared. She began to quickly focus on her predicament. She was alone in the woods around dusk with an odd man who easily could be dangerous. He obviously was having delusions; she knew for a fact that the nearest ski area (the "double bunny hill" Dad always called it) was over eighty miles away. Moreover, those mountains had been without snow for well over a month. Yet, here was a man wearing a snow suit in seventy-degree weather, professing to have been skiing. She must be cautious not to rile him. Dad always told her that when confronted with a crisis, use logic to outwit your opponent. Since running away from him didn't appear to be an option, she decided to try this approach.

"Yes," said the man. "You see, it is quite bizarre I must admit but, well, your accident gave us the opportunity to ... approach you about a little experiment."

Bethany understood nothing the man said except the word "us." There were more than one of them! She squinted to focus her eyes as dusk set in, looking for the other or others. She felt fear as her emotions welled up inside her. Holding back the tears, she bravely went on the offensive. "Maybe, maybe you want to explain all this to my father who will be here in just a moment. He always meets me here about this time."

"Your father?" the man asked, and then he smiled and began to laugh, a hearty, nonthreatening laugh. "That's a good one," he said. "Oh my dear, you must not be frightened. I mean you no harm. I don't know how to begin, yet I must. My name is Gabriel, and yours is Bethany … Bethany Anna Clarke," he said, taking a seat on the ground in front of her. "Your brother's name is Christopher, no 'Stopher,' I think you call him. Your little sister is Genny. Am I right?"

"How did you know that?" Bethany said. She looked to see if there was anyone else approaching; seeing no one, she relaxed only so slightly.

"I know a great many things, and that's why I am here," he said authoritatively.

This made Bethany a bit mad, being talked down to by a grown-up who knew no better than to wear a ski suit in seventy-degree weather. "You obviously don't know how to dress for spring," she retorted.

"Oh, my suit, eh? Well, yes, I can see how you could find my appearance unsettling. But there's a logical explanation. You see, I was skiing in the Arapahoe Basin – near Vail – you know, Colorado. Great spring skiing out there, bright sunshine during the day and blissful hot tubs at night."

Bethany knew of the area. Her dad and her uncle skied at Vail on occasion and had discussed the beauty of the nearby Arapahoe Basin – huge, majestic mountains, with thirty-foot cliffs for the adventuresome. Her father often

19

said that it was the only ski area where they post a sign "There Is No Easy Way Down," and that's the trip from the chairlifts back to the parking lot! So Bethany believed that this man had skied before, but not today.

"Well, you certainly don't change clothes very often," she said with a slight grin, momentarily forgetting her situation.

Gabriel laughed. "You are a sport! I like your character, young lady. But, indeed, this outfit and I were on the slopes just a few minutes ago."

"That's impossible," Bethany blurted, "totally impossible!"

"With me, most anything's possible," he said. "You see, I'm an angel."

Bethany was dazed. "The man speaks with such sincerity and conviction," she thought, "yet underneath his calm appearance must be a raving lunatic!" It was growing darker; she had to force the issue, subtly but with direction. "Well, I guess that would explain it. Of course, angels can fly. And since your name is Gabriel, you must be the great angel, Gabriel, who has come here to give me a message like you did to Daniel, remember?" Bethany was pleased with her recollection of one of the few things she had learned in Sunday school that year. "This will force him to deal with his fantasy," she thought.

"Oh, no! I'm not *that* Gabriel. He is truly a great archangel. Me, I'm just an ordinary angel, although I am told that we favor each other in some respects," he said, pleased with the comparison.

"You mean there is more than one type of angel?" Bethany inquired.

"Actually nine … nine 'choirs' as they are called in angelology."

"What are they?" Bethany asked, now intrigued. (Her mom always said that if a cat had Bethany's curiosity, it would need at least ten lives to survive the first year.)

"Well, from highest to lowest there's the seraphim, cherubim and thrones – they surround God whenever the Lord is resting; the dominions, virtues and powers – they're basically responsible for the stars and other heavenly bodies; the principalities – they protect the earth; and, finally, the archangels and angels – they carry God's messages. I'm just an angel, at the bottom of the totem pole," he sighed.

Bethany then realized that she had taken the wind out of his, well, his wings, so to speak. "I'm sure you're a very good angel," she said sympathetically.

"It's not easy, you know. Doing good all the time is not always fun. I'm on call twenty-four hours a day, seven days a week, fifty-two weeks a year. Doctors complain about their hours! Well, I tell you one thing, I would trade with a doctor any day! Those guys have groups to cover for them. But when God calls you for an assignment, you can't say 'God, Joshua's on call this weekend; he's rested and knows his stuff. Let Josh do it!' No way! And when's the last time you've heard of a doctor making a house call?" Gabriel contemplated a moment, "Don't get me wrong: the food and lodging are great in heaven. But I must say this assignment with you could have been better timed. It was the third day of a perfectly wonderful week's vacation – the first real vacation I've had in three years," shaking his head slowly. And the snow was so beautiful!" he exclaimed. "But, hey, this is an opportunity. I'm glad to be here. If I do a good job on this assignment, who knows, maybe I'll make archangel!"

Bethany was astonished. She was almost ready to believe him, despite her logic telling her otherwise.

"Listen, Bethany. You're a bright girl, which is good because you have so much to learn. There's a great deal of misinformation out there about God. Even angels are misunderstood. Things change. We all progress," he said.

"For example, you probably think we all still use our wings to fly."

"Well, yes, I would certainly think so," she said hesitantly.

"Do you see wings on my back?"

"No, but under your suit possibly ..."

Gabriel then took off his jacket as Bethany almost laughed at his loose-fitting, bright-flowered "Hawaiian" tourist shirt hanging down over his khaki pants. Next he lifted up the back side of his shirt for Bethany to view. "Tell me what you see."

"I ... I see two knob-like growths," she commented, inspecting them carefully.

"I haven't used my wings in over two hundred years, and without use they have simply dropped off," he interrupted. "Some other angels have kept their wings by constant use, preferring the old-fashioned way of transportation. But you just can't assume all angels have wings anymore. We angels are at least one thousand years ahead of you in technology. God, of course, is light years ahead of everybody," he chuckled. "Most of us now travel by 'JOY.'"

"What do you mean, travel by joy?"

"JOY stands for 'Journey Over Yonder,' and this little device," he said as he pulled something out of his shirt pocket, "which I am holding in my hand here, in your parlance, 'zaps' you through space at speeds up to ten thousand miles a second!" Gabriel held up the device for Bethany to see. It was the size of a very large watch face and blinked several different colors when in the "on" mode.

"Are there any side effects?" Bethany inquired, thinking that it sounded too good to be true.

"Only one, which on occasion can occur. It is the equivalent of your jet lag; some angels can't sleep for a few days after a long trip. Otherwise, the effects are quite harmless. Oh yes, and there's one more. The travel causes a brilliant light that can blind you for a few seconds, but nothing more. Here, stand next to me, and I'll demonstrate."

"Wait," Bethany responded. "I remember seeing that light and a bunch of blue butterflies. What's that all about? I mean, do the butterflies have anything to do with the travel?"

"Oh, I am glad you noticed! Striking aren't they? They are my personalized greeting. Like the blue tint? I think the color is especially sharp! I have been studying butterflies for years. Most interesting insects. Did you know that the Monarch butterfly migrates from Canada to Mexico each year, but never takes a road map and never gets lost? No one is sure how it's possible. It's a bit of a miracle you might say. One of God's many miracles."

"What do you mean, 'personalized greeting'?" Bethany asked, confused by his previous comment.

"You know, it's like choosing that little special tune for your mobile phone. We have several million insects and animals to choose from. But the butterfly is such an appropriate symbol for an angel, don't you think? Anyway, come stand by my side, and I'll show you how it works." Bethany complied, as the sun began to sink below the horizon. Gabriel then twisted and pressed a few knobs on the JOY gadget and "zap," a brilliant light flashed before them – trailed by scores of butterflies.

When Bethany next focused, she was on a cable car in San Francisco with at least three hours of sunlight left in the day. "Wow!" said Bethany. "That's incredible!" She had been to San Francisco once before with her parents and had taken rides on its famous cable cars, so she knew them well.

Gabriel smiled. He knew she now believed. "We have much to do so we must begin soon."

"Begin what?" Bethany questioned curiously. "I still don't know what this is all about."

"Let's eat," Gabriel said, changing the subject. "I'm starved. Chinese?"

"Chinese food is my favorite, especially hot and sour soup," Bethany said with a broad grin.

"You are truly an unusual girl. God has chosen wisely."

Chapter 3
The Mighty Mustard Seed

Bethany loved Chinese food but her thoughts were on other things. She knew she ordered "moo gu" something, but she couldn't even remember how it tasted. Her mind was in a whirl thinking about where she was and how she got there. "How can I ever explain this to my parents?" she quietly whispered to herself. "And why am I here?"

Gabriel read her lips. "Relax," he said. "You think too much for your own good!"

"I must know! I won't eat my fortune cookie until you tell me what's going on," she whined.

"Oh, please, anything but that," Gabriel teased. "At least open it and read your fortune. It could be interesting."

"All right. But after that you must tell me." Opening her cookie, she read her fortune out loud. "You will travel, meet a holy man and be entered in a Bible Bowl within the week," she said. "What's going on?!!" Bethany blurted out totally exasperated.

"I did that," Gabriel grinned. "Nice touch, don't you think?"

"I think this is the strangest dream I've ever had,"

Bethany mumbled, pinching herself hard to see if she would wake up.

"Oh come now, be a sport. I'm about to explain our mission. You see, you have been entered in a contest."

"A contest? What sort of contest? I don't remember entering any contest."

"You didn't, we did."

"We did?" Bethany said, looking perplexed.

"Yes, God and I entered you. Let me explain. It's a rather long story. God has been concerned, upset ... yes, even mad with the world for some time. Did you know that portions of the Bible have been translated into thousands of languages and that there are millions of copies sold or distributed to the public each year in America alone?"

"And that makes God mad?" Bethany inquired.

"No, no! Let me finish! Despite all those translations and copies, what percentage of those Bibles do you think are being read by their owners at least once a week?"

"I have no idea," Bethany said.

"Well, we angels have done some surveys, and we estimate it is less than ten percent."

"Even in America?" Bethany said, somewhat surprised.

"Your United States may be even a bit worse," Gabriel replied.

"Why?" she asked.

"At first we thought it was due to late night sports events on TV; you know, so many people staying up too late and messing up their biological sleep cycles so they are constantly tired, unable to focus on anything except their job and mindless television. Hard rock music, late-night shopping and the Internet were also explored as possible culprits, but, alas, no true pattern developed. We really don't know why. Maybe it's because Americans and others on earth are just too busy and don't think it's important or relevant. In any event, God's upset and wants to devise a program to get this Bible-reading percentage way up. So he told us angels to put our haloes together and come up with a plan."

"Wow! I never realized how much God expected of angels. You guys really have to work!"

"You bet your sweet harp we do! And if our plan doesn't succeed – how would you say it? – the Lord's not going to be a happy camper!"

"I still don't know how I fit in," Bethany said, trying to hurry Gabriel along.

"Oh yes, well, we angels thought we would pick representatives from various countries to compete in a tournament on Bible history. We intentionally would not select someone particularly knowledgeable about the Bible. He or she would have to agree to participate, of course. Over the past several months, we have been collecting candidates for God's approval. Once God approves the individual, we contact him or her, just as I have done with you."

"Listen, just because I ask a few questions in Sunday school doesn't mean I want to be in a Bible tournament."

"It's not just a tournament; it's more of an experiment really," responded Gabriel. "Each contestant will be tutored in the Old Testament by an outstanding angel, and once the contest is over, you will be sent back to your country to spread the news about God's desire to have more Bible-literate nations. If we can get you fairly knowledgeable on the Bible in a short period, just think what you can learn and teach to others over the next few years. You will be the mustard seed that spreads the word of God!" Gabriel finished.

"Wow! But what about my parents? Won't they be mad at me for not telling them where I've gone?" she said.

"God can collapse a week into a second or expand it into a thousand years. In your case, I promise that, when you return, your folks won't be mad."

"I just don't know."

"You must; you are our only child contestant!" Gabriel pleaded.

"Only child? Who are the other contestants?"

"Professors mostly, in their late thirties, early forties."

"Are you crazy? How can I compete with people my parents' age?"

"No, no. You don't understand. You see, that's your advantage! Don't you know the story of the tortoise and the bear?"

"You mean the tortoise and the hare, don't you?"

"No. That bunny rabbit concept got into the story sometime around the nineteenth or twentieth century. Now when the story first developed, back during the Dark Ages, around the tenth century – it was a bear. Bears can move a lot faster than tortoises. Of course, now that I think of it, almost any animal can. But bears often get misdirected … you know, off the track, looking for roots and berries. In fact, that's how bears got their name." Gabriel smiled.

"From berries?" Bethany questioned in disbelief.

"You have heard this story before!" Gabriel said, his grin widening.

"You know, you remind me of my father when he talks like that. I'm not certain I can trust you, but you are kind of funny."

"Hey, I'm an angel. If you can't trust me, who can you trust?" he said with a wink of his eye. "Now, how about it? Are you in the contest?"

"I don't know. Do you really think I could learn about the Old Testament? That's the toughest part."

"Guaranteed! You can learn it," he assured her. "And you can win the contest! You see, all those professor types are know-it-alls. They would rather talk about what they know than learn what they don't. So they'll almost always have their angel tutor off the track. Plus, they'll be too embarrassed to admit to their angel teachers that they are ignorant in a particular area, so they won't learn it. Finally, their minds are already cluttered with so many facts that additional information will only confuse them. You, ... you have a relatively clean chalkboard to write on. That's how I see it," he said with confidence. "You're the tortoise, and they're the bear. And remember, it's not what you know now that counts. It's what you're going to know!"

"Gee, that makes a lot of sense. It's a very logical way of looking at it," Bethany said. "All right, I'm in, although I can't imagine winning. When do we start?"

"Right away," Gabriel said gleefully. "But before we do, did you hear the one about how many students and professors it takes to change a light bulb?"

"No. I don't think so."

"One student and two professors ... the student to change the bulb, and the two professors to talk about who will write the best 'how to' book on bulb-changing!"

"Berry funny!" Bethany said, remembering the tortoise and the bear story.

"Berry funny, indeed! Your mind is quick, my dear child, which bodes well for our competition."

"You are sooo weird," Bethany said with a smile. "Are all angels like you?"

"Well, I like to think I'm rather special. Look, I may not be an archangel yet, but I'm a great teacher. And I'm going to prove it. And you're going to help me. You'll see. We're going to make a great team!" Gabriel said with confidence, as he pushed away his plate and got up to leave the restaurant.

"Ready to take a walk, my mighty mustard seed?"

"Mighty mustard seed?"

"Yes, I thought it was time to give you a nickname. And I think this one is appropriate for you, even though it is often considered a New Testament concept. You see, the mustard plant was common throughout Bible times and was very useful as an oil as well as flavoring for food. The plant could develop into a tree as tall as fifteen feet, if allowed to grow – all from a tiny seed. And I understand that it is a hardy plant which, even if subject to radiation, will, unlike most other plants, still produce non-mutated fruit. So if your faith is like a mustard seed, it will unquestionably grow many times over and in a pure form, unaffected by outside influences, producing a useful fruit for the world. I see you as a mighty mustard seed – small, strong, pure and growing. But, if you don't like it, perhaps I can think of another," Gabriel said with a big smile.

Bethany thought for a moment, "It's a little funny, but I think I like it. Yeah, the mighty mustard seed; it kind of grows on you," Bethany said with a laugh.

Chapter 4
The Salty Dog

Bethany and Gabriel strolled through Chinatown, observing its colorful buildings and interesting people. Chinatown was an exotic location in this city by the bay. The weather was cool and overcast, but streetwalkers were everywhere enjoying the brisk wind. She could smell the odor of the local fish market and hear the bells around the area as the wind made them clang in a haphazard way. A rainbow of people from all walks of life strolled past her as she reflected on what was happening. Inside her body, her heart pounded hard with excitement. At that moment Bethany felt especially alive. Multicolored hanging kites and storefront displays with oriental flair kept her mesmerized. She could hardly believe the adventure that she had begun.

While they were walking along and occasionally peering into storefront windows, Gabriel decided to begin Bethany's training. "Now, for me to educate you, I must know something about what you know. Tell me what you have learned in church," Gabriel inquired.

"Well," Bethany recalled, "in Sunday school we sing a

lot, so I know a number of Bible songs, and I've learned about Adam and Eve, Noah and the flood, Samson and Delilah, David and Goliath, and Jonah and the whale."

"That's interesting. Did you know that you have a very strong pattern of binary association?"

"Is that good or bad?" Bethany asked with some concern.

"Mostly good. Binary association is the rudimentary, that is, the fundamental element of all learning," he commented. "You see, we angels love to analyze the learning patterns and processes of people. Having studied them for thousands of years, we are quite good at it. Association by definition requires some type of linking of two things. It could be the association of a person with an event or the association of a relationship, such as the relationship of two people – Adam and Eve, Samson and Delilah, and so forth. Without basic binary association patterns, no real knowledge would be possible. Our minds," Gabriel went on, "would be cluttered with useless information that we could not use. It would be like having a bicycle with only one wheel."

"Bi-nary, bi-cycle. So "bi" means "two" and "cycle" must mean "wheels." I've never thought of it that way," Bethany said, looking very reflective.

"Oh, I could go on for hours on the subject!" Gabriel exclaimed. "We angels have studied cases where certain individuals have quaternary association patterns: 'quarter' meaning four parts, which is really only a higher pairing of two binaries. On some occasions, we even find people who are strong in trinary association. Do you know what that is?"

"Well, if binary is the association of two things and quaternary is the association of four things, then trinary must be the association of three things – tri – like tricycle."

"Precisely," remarked Gabriel. "Trinary association is a

bit less usual because most people like to think of things in even parts or sets; odd man out and all that."

Bethany was becoming a little concerned about where Gabriel's approach was taking them. "Mr. Gabriel, sir," she said trying to be polite.

"Please, call me 'Gabriel' or 'Coach.'"

"All right, Coach," she said, "this is interesting, but what does this have to do with the Bible?"

"All good things take time, Bethany. I'm getting to the point at my own speed. Remember, the bear lost the race because he was too impatient to stay the course."

"Well, I certainly feel like a tortoise right now," Bethany commented.

"Now, where was I? Oh yes, I was explaining the types of associations. The highest level of association that a person can have is macro-association."

"Macro-association? Is that like a microwave oven in reverse?"

"In a way. 'Micro' means small or short. 'Macro' means long or big. When you think of macro, think big: It's the 'big picture' approach to association. For example, when I say David, you think: David and Goliath, David kills Goliath with his sling. When I think of David, I think ... no, I see ... David's life flash before me: The shepherd boy and the son of Jesse, selected to become the king of God's people; the killer of Goliath; the musician who played the harp in King Saul's royal court and thereafter Saul's perceived enemy; David, the designer of God's beautiful temple in Jerusalem; the king who battled many people to create a strong, unified Israel; the writer of many of the Psalms; the father of Absalom – who was killed for treason against his father; and David, the father of the next great and wise King Solomon."

"Wow! You see all of that?" Bethany said, impressed with Gabriel's broad vision.

"And much more," he said with a rather satisfied smile.

"That's the difference between binary association and macro-association. Now the problem is, as I see it, nobody in the church is teaching by macro-association. Children are learning a little Bible story here, a little one there, but there's no reference point, no collective order to things – no big picture. Kids grow up to become adults and they still don't know where those stories are in relation to other stories or where to find them in the Bible. Then one day as adults they open their Bible to some book of the Old Testament and spend thirty minutes trying to find their favorite story. But they can't find it, because they're not even sure what book it's in, and they give up – sometimes forever – Bible illiterates, too embarrassed to ask for help."

"That's really sad," Bethany commented, observing the sparkling lights of Chinatown as dusk brought darkness to the streets. Nonetheless, they continued to walk and talk through the streets.

"Then there's the other group that believes that reading the Bible, especially the Old Testament, is boring and besides that, a waste of time." Gabriel went on, "They say it's not relevant anymore. Now that makes me mad! Oh, I'll admit that there are parts of the Old Testament that are extremely difficult to understand. It's like any great book – parts you want to read over and over again, other parts you just skim lightly from time to time. But, it's certainly not boring. There's adventure, intrigue, love, hate, greed, corruption, bravery, war, violence, death and miracles! Oh, I can get on a soapbox pretty quickly if I don't watch myself. Now where was I?"

("How can you stand on a soapbox?" Bethany thought to herself. "It would only collapse.") "You were talking about ... about Bible il-lit-er-ates. Doesn't that mean people who can't read?" Bethany inquired.

"Well, yes, in a fashion. You see," Gabriel continued, "Bible illiterates can read. They just don't read the Bible, either because they don't understand how to read it, or they just don't care," Gabriel concluded.

"How do you know if you are a Bible illiterate?" Bethany pushed ahead, as they continued to stroll along the streets of Chinatown.

"Good question," Gabriel said. "There is no standardized test. Incidentally, what books of the Old Testament would you look in to read about David?"

"I really don't know."

"Where in the Old Testament would you look for a good story about Samson and Delilah?"

Bethany thought hard, "I ... I don't know that either."

"How about a story about Elijah?"

"Gabriel, I have no idea," Bethany remarked as she became more and more frustrated.

"All right, here's a simple one." Gabriel paused and then said, "Where would you look for a story about Jonah?"

Bethany stopped walking and stood silently, ashamed to speak.

"God's word, child, don't you even know the books of the Old Testament?" Gabriel said, frustrated and disappointed.

"Why, no I don't. How did you know?"

"Jonah is in the book of Jonah, of course. Anyone who knows the books of the Old Testament could logically figure that one out!"

Bethany began to whimper and then cry. Tears rolled down her cheeks as she talked. "I can't help it. No one told me I was supposed to learn them. And now I'm in a contest with grown-ups, and I don't know anything!" she sobbed.

"Come, come my dear. I'm ashamed of myself," Gabriel said, placing his hands on her shoulders and looking into her eyes, "I made you cry. Forgive me, please. It's not your fault. You haven't been taught. That's all. But I'm an outstanding teacher, and you will learn the names of those books and much more. Remember, it's not what you know now that counts. It's what you're going to know!" Gabriel said enthusiastically. "Say, why don't we go for a swim?"

"That sounds nice," Bethany agreed, taking a handkerchief Gabriel had given her and drying away her last tear, "but it's almost dark."

"Don't worry, just stand next to me," Gabriel said as he pulled from his shirt pocket the *JOY* gizmo. "Let's take a little *JOY* ride, shall we?" he commented with a wide grin. Within seconds, they were zapped away.

As Bethany rubbed her eyes and blinked several times to become accustomed to the brilliant sunlight, she noticed she was standing near a tremendous lake that was almost surrounded by mountains. Translucent blue butterflies flittered around above her head. "Where are we?" she inquired.

"Guess," Gabriel said with a silly smirk covering his face.

Bethany was good at geography. She looked around and analyzed the terrain that was rather rocky and dry. "If this lake was larger," Bethany commented, "I would almost guess it was one of the great lakes, like Lake Michigan." She was generally familiar with Lake Michigan. She had visited her aunt in Chicago one summer. "But its size, along with mountains, and this rocky soil tells me I must be out West somewhere. And look at that almost foamy substance on the edge of the water." She walked over, stuck her fingers in the water and tasted it. "It's salty. Just as I had suspected. We're at the Great Salt Lake in Salt Lake City, Utah!" she cried out, extremely pleased with her analysis. "Park City is nearby, I think. My Dad says that's a great place to ski." Suddenly Bethany realized something was wrong with her analysis. "Where ... where's Salt Lake City? And the mountains look a little smaller than I had imagined," she went on.

"That city is not here because this is not the Great Salt

Lake. In fact, there were no cities here except possibly Sodom and Gomorrah, and I believe they're probably under water right over there. You see, we're in Beulah Land! Isn't it gorgeous?"

Bethany responded by looking at Gabriel with some puzzlement and confusion on her face.

Gabriel continued, "You know, God's Land of the Covenant: the Promised Land, the Holy Land! And we're at the Salt Sea in the year 1400 B.C. – or some people in your time say 1400 B.C.E. – Before Common Era. Although Moses is not here, this is the time in which he lived."

Bethany felt her heart begin to race and her knees quiver. "The Salt Sea, 1400 B.C.? Oh my God!"

"Yes, God is your God," Gabriel said. "Why do you look so flushed?"

"I'm about to have a hyperspasm!"

"Oh! Is that serious? Are you on medication? Do you wish to sit down?"

"No! No! It's just that I never thought I'd ever see it," she slowed down and counted "... almost, almost 3400 years before I was born! Oh my God!"

"We have already established that fact, so you needn't keep saying it," Gabriel said, perplexed by her constant repetition of her relationship to God.

"I'm sorry. But no one is going to believe this. This is the Dead Sea in Israel, right?" she said trying to get further assurances.

"It was called the Dead Sea later when the salt got so thick that no fish or other aquatic life could survive in its water."

Thoughts raced through Bethany's mind at a whirlwind pace, trying to put together what had happened. "So JOY is not only a travel machine but also a mini-time machine!" Bethany commented as she began to realize its full capabilities. "Like wow! This is awesome! Can I try it? "

"Technically, only angels are supposed to use it. But if you are patient, I might be able to teach you how it works."

"What about right now? " says Bethany.

"Now is definitely *not* the time. It is a very dangerous device, if used without proper knowledge," Gabriel said sternly. "Don't even think about using it without my permission. If this baby gets in the wrong hands, things can really get messed up – Big Time!"

Bethany continued to reflect on what Gabriel had told her about where she was and suddenly blurted out, "Wait a minute! I don't have a change of clothes. Do my parents know I'm here? My school always requires a consent form for trips. Don't you need to get shots for international travel?"

"Don't worry! Don't worry! Remember your parents haven't been born yet," Gabriel said. "So how can they miss you? Right? Whatever you need I will provide," Gabriel said with assurance. He then reached into his back pocket and pulled out a pile of seeds. Bethany watched with great curiosity as Gabriel examined the seeds closely and commented, "These look like they're the ones," as he selected two from the pile. Turning to Bethany he continued, "Best stand back a bit, sometimes these babies get mixed up during shipping." Gabriel then threw both seeds hard on the ground and they began to wiggle and spin in the air, rising slowly to about a foot above ground. The seeds next made soft whistling sounds before exploding into puffs of smoke. When the smoke cleared, a porcelain white bathtub with gold fixtures magically appeared, and inside the tub sat a five-foot tall mahogany-colored grandfather clock.

Bethany was very confused. Not knowing what to say, she looked straight at Gabriel for clarification. Gabriel looked back at her as he began to chuckle. "Oops, wrong seeds! These bathing suit seeds get mixed up all the time. It's *time* to *swim!* Not *bathe!*" he commented, still laughing as he pulled out two more seeds and, once again, threw them hard on the ground. This time, following whistling sounds and puffs of smoke, there appeared an array of bathing suits and towels for their selection, along with a picnic basket with food and water for lunch after their swim.

"Gee, how did you do that?" Bethany asked curiously.

"I'm an angel, remember?" Then after a pause, he continued, "OK, OK, I'll tell you, but don't expect to know all my secrets! God gives us angels a bunch of these seeds for our birthday each year. 'Party favors' you might say. Lots of fun and very useful I might add. Now, let's go for that swim!"

Bethany and Gabriel began their swim and, almost immediately, Bethany realized that this water was very different. She felt as if she was floating on the surface, and her skin was covered with salt and other minerals. Looking to Gabriel for answers, he responded, "Don't worry, this stuff won't hurt you. I'll explain it all later. Just enjoy yourself." After ten minutes of frolicking around in the Salt Sea, Bethany saw what appeared to be a small dog swimming toward them in the distance.

"That's strange," Gabriel said. "I've never seen a dog in this area before, and he certainly looks out of place in this water. Although I must say he has a rather nice 'doggie paddle,'" Gabriel commented lightheartedly as he swam next to Bethany for a closer look. As the dog approached them, it was hard to tell the color of his coat since it was covered with the salt brine of the sea. Once within their reach, Bethany and Gabriel decided to take him out, dry him off and give him some fresh water and food.

Back on land, she dried the dog carefully and was surprised how he allowed her to handle and pet him. His chocolate brown fur was thick, and Bethany decided that he was probably mostly cocker with a bit of terrier in his blood. He had a pure white spot of fur on one of his hind legs that looked a bit like a star Bethany thought. As she continued to pet him, she said, "Nice doggie. I'm not going to hurt you." Looking back at Gabriel, she commented, "Gabriel, it's such a sweet little dog. What's he doing out here in the middle of nowhere? Where are his owners? I think he has been abandoned." She then reached to pick him up and held him close to her body. "We've got to take him. He could easily die out here in this desert without our help."

Gabriel knew it was love at first sight for Bethany and this brown furry critter. "Bethany, he is cute, but I don't know. We're not supposed to pick up strays in our time travel. Maybe we could feed him and leave him some water. There really doesn't appear to be anyone around though. Let me think about it. I just don't know," he said, as he came over to pet the ball of fur. The mutt was now showing a friendly face, panting with what appeared to be a smile.

"Yes. That's a good idea. Just think about it," Bethany asserted quickly. She hoped to buy time to get Gabriel to become attached to her canine friend and agree to take him along on their trip.

"You know, his being in the Salt Sea reminds me of the Prophet Obadiah who we will study later," Gabriel commented. "It strikes me that he's not very big and possibly a bit out of place – kind of like Obadiah's book."

"Obadiah, that's a strange name. Maybe we could name this dog for a Prophet. We could call him 'Oba.' That's a cool name. Yeah, Oba, I like that." (Bethany was good at manipulating adults. She knew that if she gave the dog a name – and better yet, a biblical name – Gabriel would feel obligated to take the dog along.) "We'll just call him Oba," she said as she squeezed Oba tightly. "Now tell me more about the Salt Sea," she said trying to avert attention away from the decision that eventually would have to be made and giving Gabriel more time to become attached to her new canine friend.

"Let's eat a light snack, and then I'll start your lesson."

Chapter 5
Go West Young Lady, Go West!

After their snack Bethany wanted to know more about the geography. "Tell me about the Salt Sea, Coach."

"Well, it's a geological marvel really. It's approximately fifty miles long, north to south, and ten miles wide, and receives the waters of the Jordan River. The Jordan River begins in the mountains of Lebanon and Syria in the north and flows south to connect the Sea of Galilee with the Salt Sea." Gabriel walked Bethany closer to the edge of the water as he talked. "The depression in which the Salt Sea sits is the creation of two parallel 'faults' in the earth that produce the deepest natural depression in the world! The top of the water line is almost 1300 feet below sea level and, at the deepest bottom part, which is at the north end, is over 2600 feet below sea level."

"Wow, that's a hole!"

"Yes, it is. And did you know that in the period in which you live, the Dead Sea is seven times as salty as the ocean," Gabriel said with authority.

"So that's why I felt like the 'bob' on a fishing pole when we went swimming. I couldn't sink!"

"Precisely. Except it is probably only four times as salty as the ocean now. Come back in 3400 years and try it!"

"But why is it so salty?"

"I thought you would never ask," Gabriel said gleefully. "The Jordan River is fresh water containing only a small portion of minerals, including sodium chloride; you know, common house salt – the kind you put on a bird's tail."

"Why would you do a thing like that?"

"Ahh ... well, never mind." Gabriel said, realizing this was one expression that was not necessarily a common one for a twelve-year-old. "Anyway, this small collection of salt goes into the Salt Sea along with the water and stays there. You see, this is an inland sea – no outlet. The temperature around here can be extremely hot, so that much of the fresh water that flows into the Salt Sea evaporates, leaving the deposits of salt. Over thousands of years, the salt deposits in the remaining water have increased significantly."

"That's very interesting. How far are we from the Mediterranean Sea? Doesn't Israel border on the Mediterranean?"

"Correct. But back in these days Israel was called 'Canaan,'" Gabriel interjected. "Anyway, the Mediterranean is just about sixty miles from us, although it was called the 'Great Sea' back then, that is ... uh . . now. You tell me which direction."

"Well," Bethany said slowly recalling her prior conversation, "you said the Jordan River flows north to south and ends up in the Dead Sea – I mean, the Salt Sea. So, I guess we must be at the south end of the Salt Sea looking north, since the river doesn't come to this end. Gee, I guess the Great Sea must be to my left," she pointed with an extended arm, "which would be west."

"Excellent!" Gabriel said, impressed with Bethany's logic and sense of direction. "Now I need a paper and a pencil to draw you a map." Gabriel then reached into his back pocket, grabbed two more seeds, and threw them to the ground. They whistled and, as the smoke cleared, they transformed into a paper and pencil. Picking them up, he immediately began to draw a map of their location.

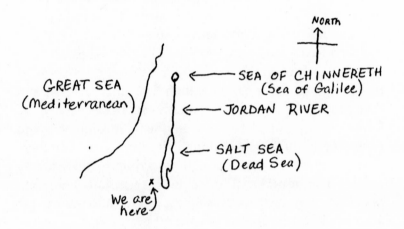

"See, that's where we are. Right here," he said, pointing to the map. "Now. What if you kept going west?"

"That's tough. I have no idea really. But I think Egypt, which is at the top part of Africa, is slightly south and west of Israel. I don't know. I imagine I would hit some part of Africa after passing over part of the Great Sea."

"Right again! Now keep going," Gabriel encouraged.

"After Africa, I guess there's the Atlantic Ocean."

"Yes, but go farther. Go west, young lady, go west!"

"Texas?" Bethany said somewhat surprised with her answer.

"No! No! Too far west. South Georgia!"

"South Georgia? Georgia is in the South. As my dad would say," Bethany paused, "don't be redundant."

"OK," Gabriel agreed. "The southern part of Georgia, maybe near the Florida line. You get the picture, right?"

"Oh … I get it. The big picture, right?"

"Right! So the next time someone asks you where Israel is, just tell them to go south to the Georgia-Florida line, hang a left, err… go east for about 7000 miles and you're practically there."

"Boy! I never realized how easy the directions to Israel would be," Bethany said with a smile, and then paused as she viewed the landscape around her. "It certainly is hot and dry here. Does it ever rain or snow in Israel?" Bethany inquired trying to get Gabriel on a different subject.

"It depends on the time of year and where you are. At this spot, it rarely rains – less than three inches a year and then only in the winter – and it never snows. Generally, the farther north from here you go the more rain you can expect, up to forty inches annually in some parts. And there is some snowfall, even enough for skiing in the extreme northern mountains bordering present-day Lebanon. Speaking of mountains, let's take a trip to one. You can get a better view from there. Here, stand beside me."

Before moving towards Gabriel, Bethany said, "I've always wanted to fly. Could we just fly there this time? You know, like Superman, the old-fashioned way?"

"Oh, Superman, eh? OK. Traveling that way is a lot slower, but sure, in this case, why not! We're not going far," he said as he adjusted his travel gizmo to its very lowest speed. Here, hold on to my arm, young lady. We are about to leap a tall building in a single bound, if we can find one!" Bethany complied, holding her newfound doggie friend tightly as they flew along the edge of the sea and slowly gained altitude moving toward the top of a mountain approximately half a mile high.

Bethany gripped Gabriel's arm tightly, as her eyes bulged at the panoramic view below. As they slowly landed on the mountaintop, Bethany exclaimed, "That was just awesome! Thanks! Hey, where are we now?" she asked, as the dog squirmed from her arms and jumped to the ground.

"We are on a mountain on the northeast bank of the Salt Sea. Now you tell me what mountain."

"Are you kidding? How am I supposed to figure that out?"

"Come on, take a guess," Gabriel encouraged. "Here's a hint: Basically, there are two correct answers and it has something to do with Moses."

"OK." She thought for a moment. "Mount Sinai," she blurted out without thinking, just to move things forward.

"Oh, excellent guess, but totally wrong. Mount Sinai has another name – Mount Horeb, and Moses got the Ten Commandments there. Mount Sinai is much farther south, way south of the Salt Sea even. I'll give you one more hint. Didn't you and your parents vacation one summer in the mountains of North Carolina?" Gabriel questioned.

"How did you know that?" Bethany said, constantly surprised at how much Gabriel knew about her and her family.

"Never mind about that," Gabriel said quickly. "Concentrate. Think of a major national forest near Asheville."

Bethany thought and thought and then it came to her, "This ... this is the Great ... the Great Smokey Mountains?" she asked hesitantly, knowing that it didn't sound right.

"No! No! It's Pisgah, the Pisgah Mountains, like the Pisgah National Forest in North Carolina!" he said, somewhat frustrated but trying not to let it show. "But you were close since Pisgah is virtually part of the Great Smokies. Pisgah means 'hill,' incidentally."

"That seems like, like ... an understatement to me," Bethany said, pleased with her rather adult comment. "What's the other name this mountain is called?" Bethany inquired, now becoming more interested.

"Mount Nebo," he said, and then continued, "and from here you can see what Moses saw when he viewed the Promised Land."

"What does Mount Nebo mean?" Bethany asked,

beginning to believe that her coach really could answer almost any question.

"Literally, it means 'mountain of the prophet,'"

"That's easy to remember, because Moses was a great Prophet," Bethany commented. "What does Mount Sinai mean?" Bethany continued, enjoying getting answers to her questions so quickly.

"Petrified peach trees! Can't you stop asking so many questions so I can finish?" Gabriel said, becoming flustered.

"It means petrified peach trees?" Bethany asked in disbelief. "I didn't think they had peach trees over here. Boy! Wait 'til I tell my aunt from Georgia! It's the peach state, you know."

"No! No!" Gabriel said, totally exhausted by his inability to move the conversation in the direction he desired. "That's just an expression I use when I get … uhh … excited." Gabriel then mused for a moment, as he considered Bethany's question. "Mount Sinai, I believe, was possibly named for the Mesopotamian moon god called Sin."

"Coach, you mean the Ten Commandments were given by God to Moses on the mountain of Sin?" Bethany said looking rather shocked.

"Why would that surprise you?"

"Well, it seems," searching for the right word, Bethany went on, "inappropriate, I think."

"I see your point. But on the other hand, it could be considered very appropriate in that without sin there would be no need for the Commandments."

"I hadn't thought of that," Bethany said reflectively. Unexpectedly, Bethany saw Obadiah running full speed toward her with what appeared to be a large bone in his mouth. He then leaped toward her, almost knocking her down. As she caught him and hugged him tightly, she commented, "Wow, this dog is some kind of athlete. Did you see that jump?" After she placed him on the ground, she said, "This is a great dog!" Oba looked at her and placed the large bone at her feet as if to indicate that he wanted to play "catch." Bethany sensed what he wanted. Picking up the bone, she drew back and hurled it as far as she could. The bone landed between two rocks and became wedged tightly. Obadiah worked hard to free it by pulling it from various angles. Bethany smiled as she watched the dog work hard to free its prize.

Turning her thoughts back to her lesson, Bethany asked, "Coach, who was with Moses when he was at Mount Sinai, and how did he get to Mount Nebo?" hoping to understand the connection of the two stories of Moses.

"Why, the tribes of Israel, of course. You do know about the tribes, don't you?" Gabriel inquired.

"Why no, I don't know any of the tribes. Is that important?"

Gabriel gazed over the land, facing the strong breeze that cooled his face only slightly on such a hot, sunny day. "Is it important? Is it important? Of course, it's important!" Gabriel shouted, feeling a sense of frustration building up again. "Now Bethany, it's not your fault, but you must understand how this makes me feel. Here you are, a child growing up in one of the wealthiest, most educated countries on earth. You have access to the city library, the county library, the state library, as well as your school's library and the Internet. Knowledge is at your fingertips. You are bright and well read. I know for a fact that you tested very well on your standardized skills test at school, and yet you tell me you don't know the name of even one tribe of Israel!"

Bethany blurted out, "How did you know about my scores ..." and then stopped, recalling he was an angel.

Gabriel walked a few feet, turned and walked back again. "This is serious, very serious. I had no idea it was this bad," he mumbled to himself. Then he turned to Bethany and, raising one arm and pointing into the air, he said, "This is my greatest challenge ever! And now I know the problem. You've only seen the ornaments. You've never seen the tree!" he said excitedly.

"I ... I don't understand."

"Bethany, let me explain." Gabriel thought for a moment, wishing to choose his words carefully. "What if next Christmas when your mom and dad got out the usual ornaments, they tell you that this year the decorating is going to be done a little differently. First, you will be blindfolded, spun around three times and told to hang those ornaments on a tree you had never seen. Oh, yes, they also tell you that the tree is between three feet and ten feet tall and that you are not to touch it except to hang the individual ornaments. How hard would it be for you to decorate that tree?"

"Why, I imagine, it would be almost impossible. It probably would take me ten times as long to do it. And the tree would look awful since I couldn't tell where each ornament was hung or how many should be used, based on the size of the tree." (Oba had finally freed the bone from its rock imprisonment. Somewhat tired by his activity, he settled down next to Bethany, as he chewed on his prize.)

"Precisely! Here's another example," Gabriel went on. "What's your favorite sport?"

"Basketball," Bethany said without hesitation.

"And who's the greatest professional basketball player of all time?"

"Jordane Licham, of course," she responded. "The absolute ultimate! Like super, super ... dudish!"

"Dudish?" Gabriel looked puzzled.

"Yes. You know, the ultimate dude. Like he's real rad!"

"Rad?" Gabriel inquired, still looking perplexed.

"You know, cool, real cool," Bethany said, hoping he knew what cool meant.

"Oh, cool," Gabriel's eyes widened. "I know the

meaning of that word. It first became popular in the 1950's or 1960's, I believe. Well, anyway," Gabriel went on, "let's imagine that somehow someone like Jordane Licham could play forever. Also imagine that the National Basketball Association had a new rule that said no one could watch basketball games in person or on television or the Internet – only radio broadcasts would be allowed. Also, broadcasters would only announce when a team scored, but not who dribbled, passed, blocked a shot or shot the ball – with the exception of the actions of Jordane Licham and a few other superstars."

"What about the newspapers and magazines?" she inquired thinking this was strange indeed.

"The same. Only statistics on how many shots were taken, steals made, shots blocked and scored, etc., would be reported," Gabriel said.

"But, Licham?"

"Yes, yes. His name could appear. So what would you think of that?"

"I think … I think Licham's got an awesome press agent to pull that off!"

Gabriel's eyes rolled. "Bethany, you're missing the point. Wouldn't it be boring after a while, even for a Licham fan?"

"I guess you're right."

"Well, see, most people's knowledge of the Old Testament is like listening to basketball on the radio under the new NBA rules. It's Moses, Moses, Moses. They know very little about the other very important players who made the team work. Now don't get me wrong – Moses and, of course, David and a few others were truly great, and I personally am a big fan of their press agents. But the story of the family of Israel, that's extremely important, too. If you want to really understand the Bible, you've got to see and feel the tree."

"That's like so rad. Tell me about the family."

"Tomorrow. Tomorrow. It's been a long day. Let's turn in early," he commented, looking toward the brilliant sunset across the Salt Sea. "Incidentally, did you know Jordane Licham used to use flubber on his shoes?" Gabriel said with a wide grin.

"You're impossible," Bethany replied as they walked toward the area where they would bed down for the night.

"Yes, but I'm sooo ... dudish!" Gabriel said, pleased with his new word.

Chapter 6
Making the Team

Bethany heard the roars of lions and the howls of wolves on several occasions during the night and slept close to Gabriel and the fire he had built to keep the animals away. When Bethany awoke, she was greeted by Gabriel's broad smile as he handed her a basket containing two pieces of barley bread, a fig cake, grapes and almonds. Bethany patted Obadiah's wooly head and then made certain that he had plenty of food before she ate her breakfast. Bethany and Gabriel, as they ate, talked for a long time about Bethany's folks, her brother and sister, and friends. Gabriel wanted to know many things about Bethany and Bethany wanted to know more about this unfamiliar foreign land that she was visiting.

After breakfast and their casual conversation, Gabriel was excited about getting back to his main subject. First, he took a moment to view the area surrounding Mount Nebo and to reflect on how much the area had changed over the years. (In 1400 B.C., Mount Nebo looked quite different than it does today. Vast hardwood and softwood trees covered the mountain and within the protection of the dense forests were wild bears, leopards, fox and deer, as well as lions and wolves. Over thousands of years, much of the trees were cut for timber or cleared for farming, except at the very highest levels, causing much soil erosion and accelerating the deforestation of the region. Today, little else but scrub trees covers much of the area – large animal wildlife has all but disappeared.) Finally, Gabriel said to Bethany, "Want to try the books of the Old Testament this morning?"

"Coach, do I have a choice?" Bethany teased, as she began to toss Oba's bone and watch him power down on his "victim" and, securing it in his mouth, return it to Bethany for another run.

"Come, come, it's really easy if you use macro-association. Anyone can learn the thirty-nine books," responded Gabriel, "if you just see the big picture."

"Thirty-nine books! I have to learn thirty-nine books!" Bethany exclaimed. "There are that many?"

"Well, that's the number the Protestants came up with for their version of the Old Testament. Incidently, if you were Greek or Catholic you might also learn the books of the Apocrypha, which would add approximately a dozen more."

"Uh-pahk-rif-uh? What's that?" Bethany asked, wondering to herself whether asking was a mistake, but unable to suppress her inquiry.

"Apocrypha literally means 'hidden.' But many Christians use the word to mean 'set aside' or 'withdrawn' from the full canonized status as scripture."

"Cannon-ized?" Bethany said with another confused look on her face. "What's the Bible got to do with a piece of military equipment?"

Gabriel could tell this was getting too complicated. "No! Not cannon, … canon – spelled with two n's instead of three – like a standard or rule. Let me explain it this way.

As you probably know, the Old Testament didn't just float out of the sky on the wings of an angel ... or a stork for that matter. It was the collection of writings that were found by certain religious men of long ago to reflect the 'Word of God.' Think of it like this: The thirty-nine books were those that made the Protestant major leagues – the canon – while the other dozen or so were good, maybe even played an inning or two, but were sent back to the minors. Those men ... err ... books are found in the Apocrypha of some Bibles but are often not given the same canonical status as the other thirty-nine. In fact, it's interesting that the word Bible comes from the Greek word 'books.'"

"So the Bible is a collection of books, and the Apocrypha are those that didn't make the major leagues, right Coach?" Bethany said, looking for approval.

"Right! That is, unless you're Greek or Catholic – they basically consider them major league players. You know, a comparison to the 'classics' would be more appropriate, now that I think of it, but you probably wouldn't relate to it as well." Gabriel then continued, "Now these books were written at different times and by different people. But the general theme of the Old Testament is the development of God's relationship with people – ultimately the chosen people, the special family, the tribes of Israel. It is also the story of the constant struggle of God's people to avoid sin and stay true to the Commandments," Gabriel looked hard at Bethany to see if she had understood.

"Well, things haven't changed very much. People are still struggling and still sinning, aren't they?"

"Indeed," said Gabriel with disappointment in his voice as he paused before making his next observation. "Fortunately, God is patient, extremely patient. And time is on the Lord's side, you know."

Gabriel continued with his comments as to the present state of things. "Things are not all bad in your world today, however. There are bright spots. There's a number of great missions that are spreading God's word. God's pleased with that. And, a few of your leaders have contributed greatly to society by developing national and international programs to foster world peace. God's very pleased with that effort as well. If only more leaders would be equally committed. Oh, well, good things take time, God always says. Now, where were we? Oh, yes, the books of the Old Testament," he commented. He then pulled from his back pocket a small packet which he proceeded to blow on, and amazingly the packet increased greatly in size and unfolded like an accordion into the thirty-nine books of the Old Testament. "These were a gift to me a few years ago from a special angel friend of mine. This pack of books is a great learning tool and very light. Plus you can organize them in any fashion you wish," he continued as he organized them as he desired and spread them out for Bethany to view. "Have you seen them presented this way before?"

"I'm not sure," Bethany said, studying the books closely.

"Well, this is a bookshelf view of the Old Testament, grouping the books together in a fashion to act as a memory aid for you. It is a quite common aid used in many churches, I understand. There is some logic to the order of the books, you know," Gabriel asserted, pausing to get Bethany's reaction.

"I have to learn all these books in order?" Bethany's voice quivered as she spoke. "That will take a lot of work!"

"Nonsense, my child. You will do it easily once I teach you how," Gabriel responded quickly, realizing Bethany needed strong assurance. "Once you know something about the organization of the Bible, this will help you to remember the books' order and generally where you are likely to find information and your favorite stories."

"Why don't they just put an index in the back of the Old Testament? Then locating something would be much

OLD TESTAMENT

LAW	HISTORY	POETRY
GENESIS	JOSHUA	JOB
EXODUS	JUDGES	PSALMS
LEVITICUS	RUTH	PROVERBS
NUMBERS	1 SAMUEL	ECCLESIASTES
DEUTERONOMY	2 SAMUEL	SONG OF SOLOMON
	1 KINGS	
	2 KINGS	
	1 CHRONICLES	
	2 CHRONICLES	
	EZRA	
	NEHEMIAH	
	ESTHER	

PROPHETS

MAJOR	MINOR
ISAIAH	HOSEA
JEREMIAH	JOEL
LAMENTATIONS	AMOS
EZEKIEL	OBADIAH
DANIEL	JONAH
	MICAH
	NAHUM
	HABAKKUK
	ZEPHANIAH
	HAGGAI
	ZECHARIAH
	MALACHI

easier." Bethany really didn't want to go through this memory exercise and was looking for any possible option.

"Excellent observation!" Gabriel exclaimed. "That would be most helpful. Bethany, why don't you suggest that to those who publish the Bible? You know, many Bibles have a form of index, but they really should be standard in any Bible publication. In any event, you really must learn these books for your contest. It's like learning the alphabet, really." Gabriel contemplated for a moment before going on, noting a little disappointment in Bethany's coconut-brown eyes. "The Old Testament is composed of the following four groups of books: the Law, the History, Poetry (sometimes called "Wisdom") and the Prophets, in that order. Can you remember that?"

"Of course I can. I'm not a doofus, you know," Bethany retorted, lowering her eyebrows and extending her lower lip as she spoke.

"You're not even a doofus I don't know," Gabriel said cocking his head to one side, with a curious look on his face, "since I don't know what a doofus is. What is a doofus? That sounds like a delightful expression!"

Bethany reflected. She never had been asked to explain the word. "It's ... it's like a dumb nerd."

Gabriel laughed uncontrollably, as he bent double and literally fell to the ground. Trying to speak through his laughter, he blurted, "Uh, what, what in the name of Abraham is a nerd?"

Bethany couldn't understand Gabriel's outburst. "They're quite common really. I have at least two or three in my class at school this year."

Trying to regain his composure, Gabriel wiped away the tears of laughter from his face. "They're ignorant sixth graders?"

"No! No!" Bethany commented as she searched for a better description. "There are two basic types really. There are general nerds and special nerds. A general nerd is someone who wears broken glasses and sticks his chewing gum under the table during lunch and then puts it back in his mouth without washing it off and does other nerdy things all the time."

Gabriel began to roar with laughter once more, as he looked for a place to sit down.

"Then there's special nerds. They are normal most of the time but have some special nerdy habit or thing they do that makes them a nerd, like someone who drinks a pint of milk in one gulp and then tries to make it come out his nose," Bethany went on.

"Stop!" Gabriel said, still laughing uncontrollably.

"That's enough! I understand!" His side ached from his howls. "Let's take a break!" he said, as he sat down in the shady spot nearby.

During the rest period, Bethany played with Obadiah and taught him a few basic tricks. Oba was a quick learner and could do "roll over" and "play dead" quite well. But her favorite trick was to have him "walk like Gabriel." This trick required Oba to stand on his hind legs and prance around as if quite pleased with himself but then suddenly fall flat on his side as he lost his balance; then he would have to jump back up and do it again. Bethany would shriek with laughter each time he fell. The dog seemed to know that he was "entertaining" her and enjoyed the attention he was receiving. At first Gabriel found the trick, because of its name, only slightly humorous, but ultimately he could not help but join in the laughter. (Since the dog learned so quickly, both she and Gabriel agreed that his owner must have worked with him a great deal before.)

Bethany thought about all that was happening and the great time she was having with Gabriel. She began to wonder whether she would be a disappointment to him or whether, like her canine friend, she would be able to perform well in her contest. She liked Gabriel so much. Her dad always said if you can't be smart, be funny; and if you can't be funny, at least be interesting. Gabriel was all three. She finally closed her eyes to rest for what appeared to her as only a few minutes when Gabriel's voice told her it was time to get on with their lesson. Rubbing her eyes, she got up and followed Gabriel to a spot nearby, ready to hear his latest lesson on the Old Testament.

Gabriel began, "OK. The Law, History, Poetry and the Prophets, in that order. Don't forget, that's our basic tree. Remember that, and you can begin to hang the ornaments. The Hebrew Bible and the Greek and Catholic Old Testament are organized a little differently but basically have the same categories. Now there are two sub-categories under the Prophets – the Major and Minor Prophets – the Minor Prophets appearing at the end, which is easy to remember. Look at the bookshelf again."

OLD TESTAMENT

LAW						HISTORY													POETRY				
GENESIS	EXODUS	LEVITICUS	NUMBERS	DEUTERONOMY		JOSHUA	JUDGES	RUTH	1 SAMUEL	2 SAMUEL	1 KINGS	2 KINGS	1 CHRONICLES	2 CHRONICLES	EZRA	NEHEMIAH	ESTHER	JOB	PSALMS	PROVERBS	ECCLESIASTES	SONG OF SOLOMON

PROPHETS

ISAIAH	JEREMIAH	LAMENTATIONS	EZEKIEL	DANIEL		HOSEA	JOEL	AMOS	OBADIAH	JONAH	MICAH	NAHUM	HABAKKUK	ZEPHANIAH	HAGGAI	ZECHARIAH	MALACHI

MAJOR   MINOR

"Notice that the entire second set of books, close to half of the total, are devoted to the Prophets of God, and with one exception that second set are all named for the Prophets. Look at how many end in 'iah' or 'el.' For example, there are four Major Prophets and twelve Minor Prophets. How many end in 'iah' or 'el'?"

"Well," said Bethany, viewing the bookshelf list, "there's Isaiah and Jeremiah and Ezekiel and Daniel – every one of the books of the Major Prophets except Lamentations."

"Correct. And Lamentations is not a Prophet. It's a book that is thrown in next to Jeremiah because it was originally believed that he wrote this book. However, many of your present day scholars believe this is probably not the case. Nonetheless, in many Bibles, it is referred to as the Lamentations of Jeremiah. Even if it wasn't written by Jeremiah, it is appropriately placed, since Lamentations means 'weeping with deep sorrow,' and Jeremiah is often referred to as the 'Weeping Prophet.'"

"You mean he was a crybaby Prophet?" Bethany asked.

"Well, not quite. Some people refer to him as the 'Chicken Little Prophet.' You get ... well, maybe we'll come back to that story later. Let's go back to the 'iah' and 'el' endings. Guess what they mean."

"I don't know. I haven't taken Hebrew or anything like that," Bethany responded, thinking that was certainly understandable for a child of her age.

"Guess. Use logic and macro-association. What other word do you know that ends in, for example, 'el'?"

"Travel?" said Bethany.

"True. But think religion, think Holy Land," Gabriel encouraged.

Finally, after almost a minute of silence, Bethany was certain she had the answer. "Israel!" she shouted.

"Outstanding!" Gabriel exclaimed. "But there is one more example that you must add to your list. How does the saying go? 'If it were a snake, it would bite you.'"

Bethany still looked puzzled.

"In the name of one of the greatest archangels ever, think child, think!" Gabriel pleaded.

Bethany's face lit up. "It's your name, Gabriel! Of course, why didn't I think of it earlier? And the word 'angel' is another!"

"Praise God!" Gabriel mumbled quietly as he closed

his eyes, folded his hands and turned his face skyward. After a short pause, he turned back to face her. "Now who would all these Prophets, the son of Isaac and several angels, be named for?"

"God?" Bethany answered almost in a whisper, fearing that her answer might be incorrect.

"You're on ... a roll!" Gabriel said with much pride. "Angel means 'messenger of God.' My name means 'strong man of God.' Isaiah means 'Jehovah (which is another name for the 'Lord') is my salvation.' Jeremiah means 'the Lord glorifies.' The American and English version of this name is Jerry or Jeremy."

"Wow!" Bethany exclaimed, "You know, the best basketball player at my school is named Isaiah. At the end of most of the games, he will shoot this awesome three-point bomb just at the buzzer, and someone always jumps up and shouts 'Do it, Isaiah!' I wonder if they realize that they are really saying 'Do it, God is my salvation!'"

"Isn't that rad!" Gabriel grinned. "Who says God can't advertise?!" Gabriel paused for a moment and then continued, "The names of the two other Major Prophets, Ezekiel and Daniel, mean 'God strengthens' and 'God is my judge' in that order," Gabriel concluded.

"Why did they call them Major Prophets?" Bethany inquired.

Gabriel pulled a Bible out of his back pocket and handed it to Bethany. "You know, a number of people died so that you could read this book. In fact, quite a few were burned at the stake or tortured for trying to make it available to the general public, but that's another story. Open your Bible to the Table of Contents for the answer to your question." (Bethany did as he requested but was uncertain how this would reveal the answer.)

Gabriel went on, "Count the pages from the first Minor Prophet Hosea to the last Minor Prophet Malachi."

Bethany counted and finally said, "Forty-eight pages, but I don't see ..."

"Now, divide forty-eight by the number of Minor Prophets – that is twelve."

Bethany answered after a long pause, "That would be four."

"Yes, the average length of the books of the Minor Prophets is just four pages long, with Obadiah and Haggai being less than two pages each. Now compare that to the Major Prophets."

Bethany counted again. After careful analysis for a few moments, she finally said, "One hundred and ninety pages, I think. And if I divide that number by four ... oops ... five, I must include Lamentations, that's –" she did her math slowly with her eyes closed as she thought it through, "– thirty-eight pages on average!"

"Now do you see why these books are called the Major Prophets? Their books are much larger." Gabriel said. "Of course, the number of pages will change based on the size of the print in the Bible you use, but the relationship in size will stay the same."

Gabriel then focused on another point. "I have divided the twelve Minor Prophets into three sets of four. Note that in the first set we have two Prophets named after God: Joel – which means 'Jehovah is mighty,' and Obadiah – which means 'servant of the Lord.' The last set has two as well: Zephaniah – which means 'Yahweh (God) has hidden,' and Zechariah – which means 'God remembers.' Thus, there is beautiful symmetry here. You have four of the Major Prophets and four of the Minor Prophets who are named for God. In addition," Gabriel went on, "the four Minor Prophets named for God are broken down so that two are in the first set of four and two are in the last set ... none are in the middle set," as he pointed to the chart.

"Oh, I get it, binary association, right?"

"Right! Very Good! And to make it even easier the 'Z'

OLD TESTAMENT

LAW					HISTORY												POETRY				
GENESIS	EXODUS	LEVITICUS	NUMBERS	DEUTERONOMY	JOSHUA	JUDGES	RUTH	1 SAMUEL	2 SAMUEL	1 KINGS	2 KINGS	1 CHRONICLES	2 CHRONICLES	EZRA	NEHEMIAH	ESTHER	JOB	PSALMS	PROVERBS	ECCLESIASTES	SONG OF SOLOMON

PROPHETS

ISAIAH	JEREMIAH	LAMENTATIONS	EZEKIEL	DANIEL		HOSEA	JOEL	AMOS	OBADIAH	JONAH	MICAH	NAHUM	HABAKKUK	ZEPHANIAH	HAGGAI	ZECHARIAH	MALACHI

MAJOR   MINOR

Prophets are both in the last set of books – just where the 'Zs' should be. Thus, with these aids and a little study, you should be able to memorize the second shelf which is probably the harder of the two."

"Maybe I could learn them in order, if I tried." Bethany interjected. "Hey, what about Samuel and Nehemiah? They are named for God. Aren't they Prophets? And they're not in the second set!"

"Pickled pigs' feet, child! That brain of yours is in … err … overdrive!" Gabriel exclaimed, delighted with her exploration of the subject matter. "Now, let's see, you were half right," Gabriel continued. "Samuel was one of the earliest Prophets, having been chosen by God to find

Israel's first king, Saul. But Samuel was also a 'judge' and his book deals more with the period of the united kingdom of Israel – all tribes had the same king. And that's why Samuel belongs on the first shelf. "

"You mean that the second set of books doesn't cover this 'united kingdom' period?"

"That's right. The second shelf of books all deal with periods following the fall of Israel's united kingdom. That is, it deals with the period where Israel was divided into two parts by the various families of the twelve tribes: The North continuing to be called 'Israel' and the South being called 'Judah.' This part of the bookshelf also covers the Israelites' captivity and forced departure from their homeland by their captors. It also includes the ultimate return of a small group of Jews – from Judah – to Jerusalem to rebuild the Temple and once again to dwell in the Promised Land."

Gabriel then thought about Nehemiah, before he spoke. "As for Nehemiah, he was a Hebrew leader and not really a Prophet. A Prophet is one who speaks for God because God speaks directly through him or her. Because of this relationship, a Prophet often also knows of future events. You see, the Prophets were trying to get the Israelites to change their wicked ways before they were severely punished by God. In fact, this is why Jeremiah was called the Weeping Prophet. He knew that God had already decided that the Israelites were to be punished by being defeated temporarily by their enemies. Some even refer to him as the 'Chicken Little' Prophet because Chicken Little was always saying 'the sky is falling and we can't do anything about it!' That is, she was saying: 'Give up to your enemies without a fight; God's already told me the outcome. We lose!' And Jeremiah said this for many years before it came to pass. Obviously, the kings of Judah weren't happy to see Jeremiah predicting their downfall. Anyway, you should now know over half the books on the second shelf. That is, all the Major Prophets, plus

Lamentations which goes with Jeremiah, the Weeping Prophet, and four of the Minor Prophets. So you only have eight more to learn," said Gabriel with pleasure in his voice.

Bethany studied the other books on the shelf. "Hey, there's Jonah, that one is easy. And next to it is Micah. You know those two go together nicely since they both are five letters long and end in 'ah,' not 'iah.'"

"Most excellent binary association!" exclaimed Gabriel, realizing that Bethany was rapidly getting into the groove of things. "Only six more to go. Listen, while I prepare lunch, you study the second shelf, and I'll test you while we eat. I tell you what, if you get them all right, I'll have a special surprise trip for you as soon as I tell you a little story about Jonah."

Bethany worked hard for her surprise trip and tested well during lunch. She had a little trouble at first with Habakkuk (pronounced Huh-bâk'-kuhk). And Malachi (pronounced Mal'-uh-kĭ) was the toughest to remember, but Gabriel gave her several memory aids – the last Minor Prophet begins with an "M." His other suggestion was that since this was the last book of the Old Testament, she should "wave goodbye to Malachi." With these aids, she never forgot Malachi again. Finally, Bethany got all the books right and asked, "So, where are we going for my surprise trip?"

"Where would you like to go?"

Bethany thought hard for a few moments, "Egypt, I think. And I'd like to see Moses."

"That can be arranged," said Gabriel. "But first, as I mentioned, I want to tell you about Jonah. You see, the book of Jonah is quite different from any of the other books of the Prophets. Unlike the others, it's not a call by a Prophet to the Hebrews to change their wicked ways but rather a story about a Prophet who was unwilling to do what God had called him to do. The 'Disobedient Prophet,' I call him."

"Oh, yeah, I know, and God had a whale swallow him for three days and then spit him out. Right?"

"You know, that's what everybody remembers about that story. But what's really important about the Jonah story is not limited to that event. Don't you remember anything else important?"

Bethany pondered the subject for a moment, hoping something would come to her. Then she responded, "I know he didn't obey God, and I think he was probably some kind of a geek from what I can remember."

"A Greek? Oh, no. He was a full-blooded Hebrew, best we can tell," Gabriel replied. "Although, possibly some of his facial features were rather Greek in nature."

"I didn't say he was a Greek. I said he was a geek!"

"What's that?"

"Don't you know anything about, about ... American culture?" (Bethany meant 'slang' but the word escaped her at the moment.)

"What's a Geek got to do with American culture?" Gabriel said with surprise.

Bethany, then realizing her error and neither wishing to admit it, nor to provide a definition for her slang word, decided it was time for a little curve ball. "Well," she started and paused momentarily, "it's pretty complicated, but I think it all goes back to the Louisiana Purchase in 1803. If I had a map, I could easily show you," she said with a smile, thinking that's the way her dad might have thrown the pitch. "But you know, it's not that important, and we really should get back to my training."

"Interesting," Gabriel mused. "You know, I knew the Cajuns were people in Louisiana who could trace their ancestry back to French Acadia, better known as Nova Scotia. The Geeks must have been a small group of settlers who moved in shortly after the Louisiana Purchase."

"Oh, yeah. That's right, I think. There're probably Geeks from all over the United States living there today,"

Bethany went on, becoming caught up in her own creation, although knowing she should abandon this little venture into the absurd.

After a moment of silence, Gabriel decided he must get back to his lesson. "I'm sorry. I let us get way off track. Where were we?" He thought hard, "Oh, yes. Jonah." Then he continued, "Well, the main point of Jonah is not that a person can be swallowed by some large sea creature and survive. It's that God wanted Jonah to go preach to the people of Nineveh and ask them to repent, and Jonah didn't want to listen to God. You see, Nineveh was the capital of Assyria – a distant land northeast of Israel – and the Assyrians were the hated enemy of the Hebrews. Yes, the Assyrian soldiers were considered brutal warriors and were greatly feared and despised by all the Israelites."

"In what country is Assyria located today?"

"You mean the period in which you live?" Gabriel asked.

"Yes."

"It's the northern part of Iraq."

"Wow! So it would be like asking a person from Israel today to go and preach the message of God and repentance in Iraq. I guess I can understand why Jonah didn't want to obey God and go!"

"For those God has called, much is required!" Gabriel responded. "It is not easy. Indeed, serving the Lord on earth is often difficult and even dangerous. We must never forget, however, that all are God's people. It was the Israelites who were first selected to show others the way. Those who are called must do all they can to assist, so that the Almighty's kingdom on earth shall soon come."

"It will take a miracle, I guess, since there's still so much hatred in the world, people still killing each other, wars and all," Bethany responded in a serious tone.

"Indeed! Possibly a number of miracles!" Gabriel replied. "But remember, with God's help, all things are possible." Gabriel sat quietly for a moment and then interjected, "Hey, let's try Egypt. Want to?"

"Sure, but don't forget our little furry friend. He's got to go too." Oba's tail began to wag with anticipation.

Gabriel thought for a moment before speaking. "Well, I guess we can't leave him here all alone. I'll have to bring him back though to find his rightful owner. But we can do that later I guess." (Gabriel was a bit concerned because, while not a prohibition, angels were discouraged from transporting animals through time. He had heard sometimes strange things had happened in transit.)

Gabriel then made the appropriate settings on the JOY gadget, as Bethany stepped to his side, scooping up the dog in her arms. The next moment, with a "zap," a flash of light and a sprinkling of blue butterflies, they were gone.

Chapter 7
Sixth Tallest Mountain

Bethany felt a little flushed by the time travel but quickly felt better and then began to focus ahead. Her eyes were still blurred, and it was almost dark. In the distance, she heard someone saying, "Welcome to the sixth tallest mountain in Texas." She looked for Gabriel who was in front of her, staring in a trance-like state straight up at the view before them.

People were everywhere and were lining up in droves in front of the "mountain" to get inside. Gabriel whispered, "This is not one of the great pyramids of Egypt. Where in the name of Moses are we? This object looks like a huge oil drill!"

Bethany surveyed the sight an instant longer and said, "We're in Texas, at … at Gusher Mountain in Gimme Land!" she declared as she began to skip around with excitement. Although this was her first trip, Bethany knew almost everything about Gimme Land from talking to her friends who had been to the world's largest kids' theme park. In fact, only a month earlier, she had persuaded her parents that her education was woefully deficient in that she was the only child in her class who had not made a trek to the great "pyramid" in the South.

"Oh my," said Gabriel looking up at the sight, "we're definitely in the wrong place. I'm afraid that I have made a little error. Maybe JOY got a speck of dust in it or something. This happens on occasion, although this is particularly embarrassing. But I can make an adjustment quite readily ..."

"Wait!" pleaded Bethany. "Can't we look around a while since we're already here? I've never been to Gimme Land before."

"And neither have I," said Gabriel, as he thought for a moment. With a twinkle in his eyes, he then roared, "Well, you know, we don't have much time, so ... let's *Rock 'n' Roll!*"

Bethany squealed with delight and then said with some seriousness, "Coach, you definitely watch too much TV – let's *Rock 'n' Roll?* Where did you learn such things?" she quipped as she looked around to find the entry to Gusher Mountain.

Gusher Mountain was where every child wanted to go. It was an amazing ride that climbed to over forty stories high with a simulated oil eruption every fifteen minutes. After whooshing through all the twists and turns, each child received a complimentary ticket for a "Gimme Bar." Gimme Bars were extra special treats filled with "fake oil" ice cream. The "oily ooze" was really a delightful thread of dark chocolate dripped to cascade down the vanilla ice cream core. But to go up Gusher Mountain, every first-time visitor had to experience the Gimme Land story, presented by the high-pitched voice of none other than the benevolent real-estate and oil tycoon, Mr. James T. Gimme, popularly known throughout Texas as "Jimmy Gimme." Bethany, Oba and Gabriel were no exception.

As the roller coaster cars passed through a large amphitheater, the story was narrated by a twelve foot tall automated Gimme Bear, who waved to the visitors with a ten and a half gallon hat. "Howdy folks! This is Jimmy Gimme, and I want to personally welcome you to Gimme Land! Keep your head, arms and feet inside the vehicle at all times, put the Gimme Ponchos on so you won't get wet and enjoy the ride. I'm about to tell you a bit about how this here property got its start."

Bethany and Gabriel's car was toward the middle and Oba, sitting at their side, looked mesmerized by the huge talking bear. Bethany said to Oba, "It's OK, Oba. This is going to be fun! Just stick close."

The talking bear continued, "I started dreamin' 'bout this place when I was just knee high to a grasshopper. Orphaned at the age of sixteen, I inherited from my fine father a small plot of Texas farmland, five acres to be exact, located here in Ragweed County, Texas." (A huge thirty foot tall screen appeared with a map of his five acre plot, showing the location of the original home and barn nearby.) "Oh, it wasn't much. It was hot and hardly any rain fell here; most people thought I should just sell it and get away as fast as I could. But I paid no attention to such talk. My father, he told me how his father and his father's father had passed down this here land. And he was darn proud to have it. He always told me, 'Hold on to my property, son. This land's special.' Well siree bob, I listened to my father and held on to that little plot. By and by, as luck would have it, glorious oil was accidentally discovered on my property and it near 'bout rained oil forty days and nights!" Suddenly the amphitheater began to shake violently.

"Hold on to your hats, kids," the talking bear began to shout, "for it looks like we've struck oil again!" The shaking gave way to a huge shower of what appeared to be oil, as the audience began to scream with excitement.

Gabriel looked perplexed as he looked up at the black

mist raining down. Bethany yelled to him, "Stick out your tongue, Coach. Stick out your tongue!"

"Why in creation would I do that?" Gabriel yelled to her above the noise of the crowd.

"I've heard about this part. The mist's got a kinda chocolate taste. It's really cool. Try it."

Gabriel began to smile and then laugh loudly as he realized what was happening. It was a visual delight as he saw the crowd of children and adults in their raingear, intermittently sticking their tongues out to capture the mist. Each child who tasted it, Gabriel noticed, would shriek with excitement.

As the audience settled down, the Gimme Bear continued, "Well, I liked owning property, and I liked oil, so with the proceeds of my oil money, I bought more property next door and, glory be, good fortune smiled on me again as I struck more oil! Before long, not only did I own the entire county where my father's original five acres lay, but I owned eleven other counties surrounding my beloved Ragweed." (Another huge color visual of the twelve Texas counties he owned flashed across the screen.)

"Gabriel, isn't this just wonderful?" Bethany turned and asked. Gabriel grinned and nodded his approval.

"Well siree, eventually, the oil wells, they just dried up one by one. And I began to think: There's not much to do around here, so I reckon I need to build something on this here property of mine, and it's got to be big! After seven years of plannin' and buildin', Gimme Land opened and as you know, 'cause of you, I got me the biggest and best kids' theme park in the world! I thank ya'll from the bottom of my heart! Oh, that sure is a mighty big mountain ahead. Have a great time!!!" the big bear said, as the mist subsided and the cars began to slowly climb to the top of Gusher Mountain.

After Gusher Mountain, almost as in a dream, Bethany, her canine companion, and Gabriel were able to whiz from ride to ride, show to show without any wait, transcending the lines of people. "Boy, this is a great way to see Gimme Land!" Bethany shouted as they barreled down Gusher Mountain for their last ride of the day.

"Yes, there are advantages to traveling with an angel!" Gabriel yelled, as his hands firmly gripped the security bar of the ride.

As they rested for a brief moment and purchased refreshments, Gabriel commented on the cleanliness of Gimme Land. Bethany told Gabriel what she had heard about the great underground workings of the theme park that made it not only clean but efficient. She went on to explain that she had heard that they had "checkers" – people who are paid by Gimme to make sure that the employees in the park are nice to people. If they weren't, it went on their record. Bethany had to ask, "Gabriel, are you a 'checker' for God?"

Gabriel laughed, "No, not really. I mean I observe people and on occasion report that information through the channels to God. But the Lord's system of judgment is extremely sophisticated and complicated. The Almighty knows so much more than we report and is so forgiving to those who truly wish to be forgiven. If a master list on people exists, it's on a chalkboard and not on some pad written in indelible ink. If you truly wish to be forgiven, your misdeeds can be erased like that," he said, snapping his fingers.

"What about miracles?" Bethany inquired. "I mean are they really true? Can only God perform miracles or can people perform them too?"

"I'll tell you what will be a miracle," Gabriel said looking directly at his Gimme Bar, "if I can finish this ice cream and answer all your questions before it melts all over me! My goodness, God sends me on a Bible history assignment, and you want theology! Before I answer your question, let me ask you a question," Gabriel said. "Was the invention of the telephone a miracle?"

"I wouldn't think so," Bethany said, "it was more of a scientific breakthrough, I guess."

"What if we took wireless telephones back with us to Egypt to the time of Moses and told the Egyptians that we could talk to each other miles apart by speaking into our hand-held devices?" Gabriel inquired. "Would the Egyptians think that was a miracle?"

"Probably so, I would imagine," Bethany said reflectively.

"So a miracle is generally an event or act that contradicts scientific laws or the laws of nature known at the time that the event or act occurs. And I would add to that," Gabriel went on, "it is often considered God-inspired or created since it cannot be fully explained. This is logical since God put us on this planet to begin with, which is the biggest miracle of all. And if you think about it, childbirth is one of God's greatest continuing miracles, for even today with all human knowledge, we don't really understand how we are put together and made to function so well. So actually God is still performing miracles most every minute of every day."

"I think that's an interesting way to look at it," Bethany interjected.

"Now on your other point, remember the Lord often works through people. Sometimes God inspires people to do some act or be involved in an event that those viewing the event at the time would call a miracle. Obviously, one of those biblical figures who performed miracles was Moses, who you should get to see soon," Gabriel said with confidence. "Do you remember the story in the New Testament of Jesus feeding the crowd of thousands of people with five loaves of bread and a few small fish, and when the people were all fed, the baskets containing the loaves came back to the disciples full of broken pieces of leftover bread? Would you consider that a miracle?" Gabriel asked.

"Well, yes, I definitely would!"

"What if I were to tell you that most of these people in the crowd were extremely poor and, although they generally didn't know each other, they were so inspired by Jesus' word that those who had brought a small bit of bread and other food with them were willing to share with those in the crowd who had none, so that there was enough to go around. Would that be a miracle? Before you answer, also assume that most of the individuals who shared their own bread may not have been certain that they would be able to feed themselves or possibly even their family members for the following week."

"Well, I imagine ..." Bethany said as she assessed the situation.

"And, would it make a difference if I told you that there was a wealthy baker who, although he had never done anything for anyone but himself, was so inspired by Jesus' message that he quietly passed out loaves at the back of the crowd so that all could be fed?" Gabriel asked.

Bethany reflected deeply and then spoke, "I think I see your point. At first I thought it was a miracle. Then I thought it wasn't because I could understand how it might have happened. You know, the more I think about it, the more it would seem to be a miracle."

"Why?" said Gabriel

"Well, it's hard to say, but, for example, it seems to me that whenever someone who unexpectedly is doing God's work, and this causes a great event to occur that can't be explained, then it's probably a miracle!"

"Very well stated, indeed!" said Gabriel, with a broad smile on his face. "God performed incredible miracles creating the world and making the world function so well as it does today. There can be no question as to the Lord's powers and ability to perform miracles. The important point is that, with the help and inspiration of God, people also can accomplish wonderful, unexpected things in ways that today can't be readily explained."

"Wow!" Bethany said, quite impressed with Gabriel's explanation. "You sure know a lot about these things. By the way, what really happened with Jesus and those loaves of bread?"

"Very simple. Jesus made the bread and fish multiply, of course. No doubt about it! But I wanted you to realize that miracles can still occur today, especially when people focus on God's work."

As Gabriel finally discarded his rapidly melting, double-dutch-chocolate ice cream cone, Bethany spotted a rectangular piece of paper on the ground and picked it up. "A Gimme Dollar!" she yelled. The dog sniffed the dollar as Bethany began to pick it up.

"This place has its own currency?" Gabriel asked in amazement. "Isn't it part of your United States?"

"Officially, I think it still is," Bethany said. "But my dad says it's just a matter of time before Gimme Land gets some official independent status. He says the people at Gimme have been talking to those people at the Vatican to see how these things are done."

"The Vatican in Rome, Italy, where the Pope lives?" Gabriel's brows raised, intrigued by Bethany's statement. "What does Gimme Land have in common with the Vatican?"

"Well, I don't really know that much about it, but my father says that Gimme Land is secretly planning to build the world's largest airport on its grounds using super quiet jets which will literally drop you off at your hotel, all within the park, of course. Smaller international airports would be built at Gimme's overseas operations. You know, lots of people who work at Gimme Land are foreigners, and they expect to sometimes have people shortages at different locations. Dad says, if they can streamline the visa and customs process, they can transport their people more efficiently, along with any paying customers, of course. Plus, they are focusing on the global parent market."

"What's that?" Gabriel inquired, bewildered by the whole idea and Bethany's apparent understanding of it.

"Oh, that's just another way of saying that everybody's parents – the Americans, the Europeans, the Asians, the Africans and the Australians are traveling to each other's country on business on a regular basis. The dad's in Tokyo while the mom's in Johannesburg. You see, parents need a convenient, exciting place to meet their kids for a few days of relaxation between business trips. Later on, with more air travel required by their jobs, parents will consider moving closer to airports and Gimme will be ready!"

"What do you mean? Gimme will be ready for what?" Gabriel said, totally confused.

"The next stage after that is to develop permanent residents and apartments directly on Gimme property. These living quarters along with huge shopping malls on the properties will be all it takes. Dad says global parents would line up in droves for the chance to be near the airport, have their children at the most exciting playground in America and have their property managed by world-class planners. And that's where the Vatican comes in."

"It does?" Gabriel said with amazement.

"Yes, to do this and to do it right, Gimme can't be subject to state, local or even federal zoning restrictions. Dad says Gimme knows that the bureaucracy will kill creative plans and not be cost effective. So you see, Gimme must make its major theme parks, such as Gimme Land, independent from government meddling – just like the Vatican."

Gabriel looked straight at Bethany and said, "Are you sure you are just twelve years old?"

"Why of course I am! Why do you ask?"

"Oh, I'm just trying to figure out how long before you

are going to explode onto the business world," he mused. "We should be going now, Egypt awaits!" Gabriel adjusted the time machine to what he hoped would be the right setting and motioned to Bethany and Oba to stand close by. In an instant, they were gone – leaving Gimme Land a farewell gift of a stream of brilliant translucent-blue butterflies to enjoy for a fleeting few moments.

Chapter 8
Up the Tree Goes the Family

Gabriel stood firmly with his feet wide apart, hands on his hips, as a large smile broke across his face while he viewed the vast desert. "This is it – the land of Goshen in Egypt and just over there, along with the Nile is the city of Rameses. You know, Rameses and the city of Pithon, which are farther east, mostly southeast from here, are two of the 'store cities' built by the Hebrews during the period that they were slaves in this land. Store cities were where the Egyptians kept military and other supplies in case of war. You can read about Goshen in Exodus 1:11, as I recall."

"Hey, I remember when I lived in Connecticut there was a town called Goshen. Was it named for this place?"

"Could have been," Gabriel said and then continued. "There's a number of towns in America and elsewhere that were named after biblical sites or towns. Of course, Goshen, Connecticut, could have been named for another biblical Goshen located south of Judah in the hill country near the Negeb – which means 'south,' incidentally." He then began to draw a map on a piece of paper pulled from his back pocket. "This Goshen is referred to in the book of Joshua. I seem to remember a Goshen, Indiana, also. Yes, indeed, there is a Goshen College there as well, I believe," he said as he completed his rough map of the area.

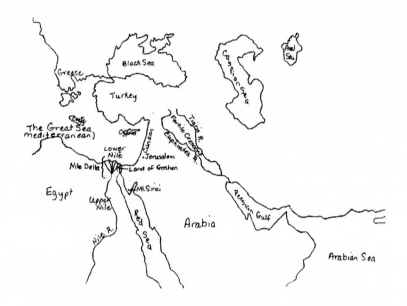

Bethany viewed the roughly etched map as Gabriel pointed out each place of interest. "Coach, I think you've made at least one mistake," she said with some authority, "and I hope you don't mind if I point these things out to you."

"Not at all," Gabriel responded, "I've made plenty before, so go ahead."

"Well," Bethany went on, "you see that funny little upside down triangle area – I believe you called it the Nile delta area – with the upper Nile at the bottom and the lower Nile at the top of your map. That's backwards, isn't it?"

"No. Although, I can see your point. The Nile flows from south to north. It's one of only a few major rivers of the world that does that, I believe. So, anyway, the upper

Nile is closer to the beginning of the river, and the lower is near the end of the river, where it flows into the sea. This point is what we call the 'mouth' of the river and its most fertile part."

"Gee, that is rather confusing. Anyway, I have another question," Bethany continued. "You mentioned Hebrews being in Egypt. What's the difference between a Hebrew, a Jew and a Gentile? And what were the Hebrews doing in Egypt anyway?"

"Good questions!" Gabriel paused, reflecting on how to answer. "This is not easy to explain unless we get into some detail, but it is important, so let me take my time and elaborate fully. Here, you and Oba sit down beside me and be comfortable in the shade of this rock. Let me draw you another map," he said, again drawing on a piece of paper pulled from his back pocket a somewhat simplified family tree. After about ten minutes he had completed his task.

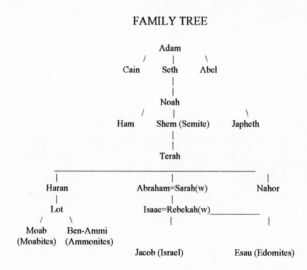

FAMILY TREE

"Note that the broken lines under the tribes of Israel mean that I skipped generations, but obviously I can't include everyone," Gabriel said, pleased with his production. "We're focusing on the 'big picture' you know."

"Wow! You even have Jesus on your chart," Bethany exclaimed. Hey, why is he on this map anyway? God was his father – not Joseph!"

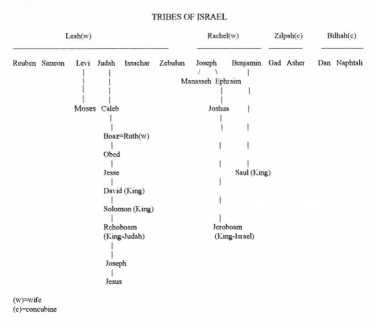

TRIBES OF ISRAEL

Leah(w)						Rachel(w)		Zilpah(c)		Bilhah(c)	
Reuben Simeon	Levi	Judah	Issachar	Zebulun	Joseph	Benjamin	Gad Asher	Dan Naphtali

(w)=wife
(c)=concubine

"Well, Joseph was as close to a human father as Jesus could have. Let's call him Jesus' step-father and leave it at that. But remember that the Old Testament Prophets had predicted that a savior, or in Hebrew – the 'messiah,' would come from the family of King David of the tribe of Judah. So this was considered pretty convincing evidence to some Jews that he was the one everyone was waiting on. In addition, Jesus' mother, Mary, and her side of the family can be traced back to King David also. Anyway, the problem was that most Jews expected a more traditional king – you know more of a 'warrior king' – and Jesus didn't fit that mold at all."

"Coach, how do you remember all this stuff?"

"Practice," he responded, "For example, I can do these charts in my sleep. It's, how do you say it? 'No sweat.' And if I forget, I just look it up. Most of the basic Old Testament genealogy is covered in Genesis 5 and 10 and in Matthew 1. Or, if you really want to get into the details of family history, check out 1st Chronicles, Chapters 1 through 9. It's just like your folks keeping a family tree and telling you who was related to whom and which of your grandparents did what. The Hebrews thought this was very important. Now, where was I?" Gabriel's eyes rolled toward his brows and his right forefinger rubbed across his lips as he reflected. "Oh yes, most everyone knows that Adam and Eve had Cain and Abel, but they also had a son called Seth who had a child, who had a child, who had a child, and so forth and so on until Noah was born. You know, the guy who liked to collect animals for his boat," Gabriel chuckled. "Anyway, Noah had three sons – Shem, Ham and Japheth, who represent the three great divisions of the human race as known by the early writers of the Bible."

"The descendants of Shem lived as far south as southern Arabia and as far north as the lands between the Tigris and Euphrates Rivers. This area includes many of the people who live in the present day countries of Israel, Jordan, Saudi Arabia, Iraq and Syria. These people were called 'Semites' since the Greek-Latin spelling of 'Shem' was 'Sem.' On the other hand, Ham was the father of the Egyptian people and Japheth was the father of the Persians ... err ... the Iranians. So you see, to say that the Arabs are anti-Semitic or 'against Shem' is somewhat of an oxymoron."

"Oxy-what?" Bethany inquired.

"Oxymoron, oxy means 'sharp' and moron means 'dull' ... sharp-dull, get it?" asked Gabriel.

"That doesn't make any sense," Bethany commented.

"Precisely!" Gabriel said with emphasis, but then was silent as Bethany looked at him still a little confused. "You know," Gabriel elaborated, "they're word combinations that are contradictory or don't logically go together, like 'cruel kindness.'"

"Oh, I get it, like 'smart boy,'" Bethany grinned.

Gabriel smiled as he shook his forefinger as if to say naughty, naughty. Then his head turned and his eyes roamed across the sky as he mused over his subject matter, before returning to the family history lesson. "OK," Gabriel continued. "Now Shem had a child, who had a child, who had a child and so forth and so on until Terah was born. Terah grew up and had three sons, the most important of whom was Abram, before his name was changed to Abraham."

Bethany couldn't help herself, she had to ask, "Why was his name changed to Abraham? I mean they didn't have Hollywood back then and, if he was trying to hide from someone, that name change couldn't fool anyone."

"Oh, no. It was nothing like that. God changed his name. He did a lot of that to Abraham's family. Abraham's wife's name was Sarai, and he changed it to Sarah. Abraham's grandson's name was Jacob and God changed it to Israel, but we're getting ahead of ourselves here."

"Israel, so that's where that name came from!" Bethany said with great excitement. "Why did God do that anyway?" commented Bethany looking a bit puzzled.

"You've heard of born-again Christians? These people were born-again Hebrews! God had touched their lives and their name change was constant evidence of their devotion to the Lord Almighty."

"Hey, wasn't it against the law or something to go around changing people's names? I mean, would the government allow that to happen?"

"To the Hebrew people, God's law was the law," Gabriel commented. "Anyway, think about it, the Lord often travels faster than the speed of light, but have you ever heard of God getting a speeding ticket?" Gabriel said, half-joking.

"Well, no. That's a good point, I guess," Bethany said with a smile. "But you still haven't explained why Abraham was a Hebrew. All I know is how he was a Semite, a descendent of Shem," Bethany said impatiently.

"Suffering seaweed! Child, Jerusalem wasn't built in a day!"

"Is the phrase 'suffering seaweed' an oxymoron 'cause I really don't think it makes any sense," Bethany inquired. "How can seaweed suffer?"

Gabriel gasped, a little flushed in the face, and then held his breath and silently counted to ten to gain his composure. Trying to stay calm, he said, "Might I remind you that your constant inquiries can impede development of consistent thought processes ..."

"Isn't that another oxymoron?" Bethany interrupted. "Because if I don't ask questions, how will I ... ?"

"Never mind! Never mind! Let's move on," said Gabriel, not wishing to debate this twelve-year-old "sweet juggernaut." "Now, where was I? Oh, yes. The Bible says that Abraham lived in Ur. Many scholars believe that this was the town not too far from the intersection of the Tigris and Euphrates Rivers before they flow into the Persian Gulf."

"Wait a minute," Bethany said, "wouldn't that make his family originally from Iraq?" recalling her geography lessons from school.

"Why, yes, I guess you could say that."

"Boy, I never would have guessed that!"

After a pause, Gabriel continued, "Well, anyway, then Abraham and his wife, Sarah, along with his brother, Nahor, and his nephew, Lot, moved to Haran, a town in present day Syria. And the Lord said to Abraham in Genesis 12:1-3:

> ... Go from your country and your kindred
> and your father's house to the land that I
> will show you. I will make of you a great
> nation, and I will bless you, and make your
> name great, so that you will be a blessing. I
> will bless those who bless you and the one
> who curses you I will curse; and in you all
> the families of the earth shall be blessed.

"So, being a man of great faith and with such a promise from God, Abraham moved from Haran to the land of Canaan – basically the area where present day Israel and part of Jordan are located. And in one of the first places in Canaan Abraham stopped, God told him that this was the land that was being given to Abraham's descendants. Abraham then built an altar to God as a way of showing his thanks for this gift," Gabriel continued. "In Abraham's travel he probably had to cross over a number of bodies of water such as the Euphrates River in Mesopotamia or possibly the Jordan River that connects the Dead Sea and the Sea of Galilee. You do remember seeing the Jordan River, right? Anyway, in Genesis 14:13, Abraham is referred to as the 'Hebrew' – which probably means the 'one that crossed over'. My best guess is that he was called Hebrew because he was an outsider in the land and had crossed over some river or other significant barrier to get there."

"You mean you're not certain?" Bethany said with great surprise.

"I'm an angel, not an archeologist," Gabriel commented, matter-of-factly. "God doesn't tell us everything. We have to figure a lot out for ourselves."

"So I'm still not certain I have the right answer after all this! Holy Samolee! Gabriel, why doesn't God just tell you these things!"

"God tells me what I need to know. God doesn't

believe in 'spoon feeding,' – you know, giving information on demand. You've got to work with the Lord. Anyway, figuring certain things out for yourself can be a lot of fun. Plus, we've got lots of resources – people, books and all. So I believe that learning about God and the Bible is a constant endeavor. God's so interesting you never tire of the Almighty's word. Through prayer, I talk to the Lord lots of times each day. And I get good advice. But I'll never figure everything out or not need to pray."

Gabriel paused to reflect on whether he should say anything else on the subject and, finally, after several moments he continued, but looked up as if in a deep spiritual state. "Sometimes I go to God, not for answers but just for understanding. You know, like when you go to your mom or dad and want them to hear how your day was. And you feel better just because they listened. God's a lot like that. And at some point when you need to hear the Lord, if you listen really hard, the Almighty will tell you what you need to know. I guess God smiles at me a lot and probably laughs at some of the silly situations I get myself into. But God's never, never unkind, and the Lord's door is always open if you just knock."

Bethany focused on Gabriel intensely, sensing that he was sharing a great deal more than Bible history with her at the moment. Suddenly Gabriel turned toward her and looked directly into her eyes. "You do knock, don't you Bethany? You know, pray to God? Always talk to God at least daily. If you don't, you'll be missing out on the best relationship you could ever have. That one relationship can make all your other relationships much, much stronger. That's pure joy, Bethany. And don't just give the Lord lip service – saying something without reflection or feeling. I mean, really tell the Almighty things about your life and ask for help when you need it. God's a great listener and a great friend. Don't forget that Bethany. It's important. OK?"

"OK, I won't forget," Bethany responded with sincerity in her voice.

Gabriel then realized that he had probably said enough to her at the moment about prayer and turned back to the lesson at hand. "Now, you also wanted to know the difference between a Hebrew and a Jew. Let me see ... technically speaking, a Jew is a Hebrew who happens to fall in one line of the Hebrew family tree." He unfolded his family tree chart created earlier. "As I believe I mentioned, Abraham had a son named Isaac and Isaac had twin sons, Esau and Jacob. From Jacob, whom God named 'Israel,' we get references in the Old Testament to the twelve tribes of

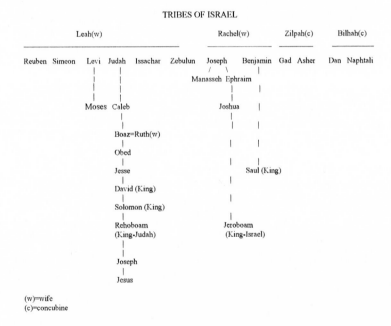

TRIBES OF ISRAEL

Israel. Look for the twelve sons named under Jacob's name and then find the son named 'Judah,'" Gabriel said, pointing to the chart.

"Look underneath Judah's name and, for example, you will see down the line King David's name. David was a Jew in the truest sense in that he was a descendant of not only

Abraham the 'Hebrew' but of Judah the 'Jew.' And the religion became known as Judaism because most of the other tribes, for all practical purposes, disappeared from the Promised Land, which we will discuss later. In most cases, Hebrews and Jews are either the same or are kissing cousins. Nonetheless, for a period of their history, certain of the tribes fought each other like cats and dogs. On the other hand, Gentiles are non-Jews. That's fairly straightforward. Although, I can think of one exception."

"What's that?"

"Well, there's at least one place in the U.S. where Jews are apt to be called Gentiles whether they like it or not," Gabriel observed. "Want to take a guess?"

"May I ask some questions?"

"Sure."

"If I were in this place, would I be considered a Gentile?"

"You don't attend their church, so, yes, you would."

"Oh, so it has to do with some other religious group. Right?"

"Correct! Very good, Bethany! Very good. Now go on."

"Well, I know a lot of Presbyterians and Baptists, and I've never heard them call a Jew a Gentile, so it must not have anything to do with them. I'm not sure about the Catholics or the Episcopalians. Does the reason these people call the Jews 'Gentiles' have to do with how many children they have or how much wine they drink or something like that?"

"Nope. But alcohol or, I should say, the prohibition against drinking it, is a clue."

Bethany thought for a moment and then asked, "What does the word 'Gentile' mean anyway?"

"It means literally the 'same tribe or race.' It's a French-Latin word."

"Oh, I see, so Jews could be considered Gentiles since they are from the same tribe kind of, aren't they? But they're not Gentiles with non-Jews. I mean like they really are Gentiles who happen to be Jews. Boy, this is getting confusing!"

"No question, it's difficult to understand fully." Gabriel responded. "Let me help you a bit. You see, the word Gentile is really a very imprecise word ... that is, it has numerous and almost conflicting meanings depending on who is using the word. For example, the early Christians used the word Gentile to mean anyone who did not believe in God. You see, most of the Romans still worshiped the gods of nature and so they were referred to as Gentiles. Think of it as a term used to separate yourself or your group of people from all others ... from all other tribes or clans. Now what religious group in the U.S. considers itself quite different from all others and, to a degree, dominates and runs the activities of a major city in the U.S.?"

"The Moravians?" she said. (She thought they were a bit different from other religious groups and made a Christmas star that was quite beautiful and unusual, and a big money maker she guessed. Her parents had bought one on their family visit to a Moravian village just outside Winston-Salem, North Carolina.) "Gee, I didn't know they ran Winston-Salem!"

"They don't. Well, at least the last time I checked they didn't. I'll give you some more hints. What major city in the U.S. is near a river named Jordan which flows into a salty lake and backs up to the Wasatch Mountains? It also has great skiing nearby, and the people who live there generally don't drink or smoke."

"Oh, is it Salt Lake City in Utah? And isn't that where all the Mormons live?"

"Well, yes, quite a few. And Salt Lake City is the Mormons' headquarters ... their 'Jerusalem' or 'Zion,' so to speak. If you ever go there, you should definitely see the Mormons' great temple. It took them forty years to build, and it really is exquisite. Anyway, the Mormons refer to anyone who is not a Mormon as a 'Gentile.'"

"So to a Mormon, a Jew is a Gentile and to a Jew, a Mormon's a Gentile. That's cool!" Bethany exclaimed.

"Now, where was I?" Gabriel said. "Oh yes, I was going to explain how Moses and the Hebrews got into Egypt."

"Yes, you were talking about Abraham, and how God promised Abraham that he would be the father of a great nation if he would move to Canaan," Bethany commented, trying to refresh his memory.

"Well, things were tough on Abraham at first. The Canaanites had been in there for quite some time and had built towns and cities throughout the area. It was pretty clear that, although God had agreed to give this land to Abraham's descendants, someone forgot to tell the Canaanites! So Abraham and his family were living a rather nomadic life in tents and trying to stay alive in a country where they were surrounded by people who didn't like them. Besides, the Canaanites already had their own gods, and they weren't about to accept Abraham's 'one and only God' religion. Incidentally, the Canaanites' main god was Baal, and the major female god of the Canaanites was called Ashtoreth. Anyway, Abraham's family was horrified by the Canaanite religious practice of making 'Baal sacrifices' and 'foundation sacrifices.' Foundation sacrifices were especially dreadful. This practice involved inserting the body of a sacrificed child into the wall or foundation of the house to bring good luck to the remaining family members."

"Get real!" blurted Bethany, as she closed her eyes and covered her ears in shock and disbelief.

"I'm not certain how I can do that," Gabriel said, "but I'll try if you explain …"

"No! No! I mean, that's not true is it?"

"Best I can tell, it is. You see, people in those days had little respect for human life. Now you know what God was up against, and how important it was to find people who would learn to follow God's ways. In fact, there's a Bible story on sacrifice that I would like to share with you, because I think it is often misunderstood." Gabriel tapped lightly on his lips with his forefinger as he tried to organize his thoughts. "Now Abraham had a son by his wife, Sarah, at a very old age. Sarah and Abraham had wanted a child for many years. A child was born to them appropriately named Isaac, which means 'laughter' or 'to laugh' in Hebrew. You see, both Abraham and Sarah laughed when God told them that they were going to have a child. They thought they were much too old for that. Well, after Isaac's birth, Abraham could not have been happier. He loved Isaac as he did no other. Then one day when Isaac was a young lad, probably a bit younger than you, God decided to test Abraham by telling him to take Isaac and sacrifice him as a burnt offering on a mountaintop. Genesis 22, I believe."

"I remember that story, and just as Abraham was about to take his son's life, God's angel stopped him," Bethany recalled. "I always wondered why God tested Abraham like that. It seems rather cruel to me."

"Remember," observed Gabriel, "child sacrifice may have been a standard practice in the Canaanite community. I believe that God was saying, in a way, that while the Lord requires complete devotion, human sacrifice, as was practiced in the Canaanite religion, is not required or desired."

"Boy!" said Bethany. "If I were a Canaanite child, going to church or moving to a new house would have been a scary experience!"

"Ahh … right," responded Gabriel. "Now, let's see. So Isaac and Rebekah had twins, Esau and Jacob. Because Esau was born a few minutes before Jacob, Esau was technically the older. Therefore, Esau, as the first born son, was entitled to a 'double share' of all of his father's property upon his death, according to the laws of the time."

"Gee, that doesn't seem fair that the oldest son gets so much more," commented Bethany, as she picked up a stick to draw in the sand, but listened attentively to Gabriel's story.

"Well, Isaac's wife, Rebekah, also thought it was unfair. And since she favored her son Jacob, she helped him take his brother's birthright by cooking a good meal for his father. Why don't you read about it while I fix us lunch? It's Genesis 27:1-40."

Chapter 9
A Few Good Kids

Bethany read the verses as Gabriel suggested during her lunch break along with a number of other Old Testament verses. She made sure that her dog was well fed and well exercised. She had come up with a new game for him. She would run along calling for him to jump on her shoulder with his prize bone in his mouth. Next, while momentarily on her shoulder he would hand her the bone "baton" and immediately leap forward as she threw the bone as far away as possible. Of course, Oba would retrieve the bone and continue to do the trick over and over again until they both were exhausted.

After the games with Obadiah, Bethany was ready with a question for Gabriel. "That's a great story in the Bible about Jacob, especially where he makes his hands look hairy like his brother Esau's hands," Bethany asked. "I just want to know one thing. You remember where Isaac wants some food and Rebekah tells Jacob to 'go fetch two good kids' so that she can prepare them for his father, she's not talking about … about, you know. I mean kids aren't …."

"Kids? Oh my, no. Kids are young goats!" Gabriel said

as he began to howl with laughter. "Now I know why you hardly touched your lunch, dear child."

"Well, I didn't know for sure. And my stomach did feel kind of funny," Bethany went on, "but I feel much better now. Boy! I bet Esau was mad when he figured out that Jacob had tricked him out of his birthright. Why didn't they just split the property right down the middle? That would have been the fairest thing to do."

"Undoubtedly," said Gabriel. "But things didn't work that way back in those days. Anyway, you're right about Esau being furious. He threatened to kill Jacob, and Isaac ordered Jacob to go to the village of Nahor, which is near the village of Haran. As you will recall, Haran was that town in Syria almost 500 miles northeast of Canaan, where Abraham had lived for years but then left to come to Canaan on God's instructions. This was to be a temporary move for Jacob, just until things blew over. And his mother, Rebekah, wanted Jacob to find a nice girl from this area to marry – Rebekah was from Haran, you know. She thought the Canaanite women were just awful. Anyway, Jacob did go and found a wonderful wife named Rachel, although he had a few problems with her father, Laban."

"Hey, wasn't Jacob the one who had that dream about angels going up and down a ladder? And didn't he fight with an angel?" Bethany asked, remembering a recent Sunday school lesson.

"Correct," said Gabriel. "That happened in a place he named Bethel. Do you know what 'Bethel' means?"

"The ending 'el' means God, right?" Bethany stated with some confidence.

"Correct. And 'beth' means house, so Bethel means house of God," Gabriel said. "Well, anyway, the Lord spoke to him in his dream and said in Genesis 28:13 through 14:

> ... I am the Lord, the God of Abraham your
> father and the God of Isaac; the land on

which you lie I will give to you and to your offspring; and your offspring shall be like the dust of the earth, and you shall spread abroad to the west and to the east and to the north and to the south; and all the families of the earth shall be blessed in you and in your offspring.

"In essence, God was repeating the covenant – that is, the promise – to Jacob, which God previously made to Abraham and to Isaac. Well, anyway, Jacob sometime thereafter returned to Canaan and had twelve sons: Reuben, Simeon, Levi, Judah, Issachar, Zebulun, Joseph, Benjamin, Gad, Asher, Dan and Naphtali," Gabriel said, counting them off on his fingers. "You see, God had changed Jacob's name to Israel, which, incidentally, means 'he struggles with God.' And each of Israel's sons represents a separate tribe that received property in the Promised Land, with two exceptions that we'll get to later. In any event, Israel's son Joseph was the first to go to Egypt."

"And Moses was a descendant of Joseph, right?" Bethany interrupted, hoping this was the missing link to finally get to Moses.

"Not quite. You see, Moses was a descendant of Joseph's brother, Levi," Gabriel added.

"You mean Levi's like the jeans people?" Bethany asked, using her memory by association. "You know, Coach, I can always remember Moses was from Levi's family by thinking of him walking around in the desert in jeans. Pretty silly, huh?"

"If that's the way you can remember, more power to you. Incidentally, I wear jeans on occasion, especially when I horseback ride."

"You horseback ride?" Bethany inquired, for some reason surprised.

"Yes, I love horses," he responded, "and old cowboy

movies. When I have time, I really enjoy watching old reruns of Bonanza."

"Bonanza? Is that like Jeopardy?" Bethany asked curiously.

"No. No! Bonanza, you know, the Cartwright brothers: Adam, Hoss and Little Joe. Now that's family entertainment! Did you ever see the one where Candy, the hired hand, inherits stock in a real estate company? He doesn't know that the company is swindling money from naive easterners in New York for worthless desert land. Hoss and Little Joe have to help Candy understand that he can't accept the tainted fruit."

"I don't understand," Bethany responded. "If it's desert land, how could you grow fruit? Anyway, who would want to eat painted fruit? It sounds awful!"

"Tainted fruit! Not painted fruit! Fried freckles child, don't you hear well?" Gabriel asked.

"I hear well enough," she retorted, "to know that fried freckles is a disgusting term. Yuck!"

"You're right. I'm sorry. It was an unfortunate choice of words, especially with your lunch situation earlier. I don't know what came over me." Gabriel then viewed the desert landscape and gave a faint whistle. Far in the distance appeared a magnificent white Arabian horse galloping toward the two of them. As the horse approached, Gabriel asked, "Do you know how to ride?"

"A little. I took horseback riding in Connecticut for two years," Bethany responded.

As he climbed onto the large active stallion, Gabriel shouted, "Good, give me our best friend" (referring to Oba) "to hold and just grab my arm. I'll pull you up for the ride of your life!"

"But, I ... I usually have a saddle," Bethany said with uncertainty in her voice, but before she could say anything else, Gabriel had her arm and threw her on behind him.

"We're off!" Gabriel yelled as the huge white stallion

reared onto his hind legs and with a bolt took off into the desert toward Rameses. Bethany grabbed on to Gabriel like a hungry boa constrictor holding its prey. As she gained confidence to open her eyes, she experienced the feeling of near flight. The stallion spread over the desert terrain as if he had wings. Bethany was enjoying the ride so much that she didn't want it to end. Finally, however, the horse came to an abrupt halt. When the desert dust settled, Bethany viewed for the first time the ancient city of Rameses.

After they dismounted, Gabriel told Bethany to sit down outside a modest home of bricks made from mud, chopped straw, palm fiber, small pieces of charcoal and shell. As they waited, Bethany asked, "Did the Israelites help build the pyramids? Are they near here?"

"Good heavens no! The pyramids were built years before the Israelites were here as slaves. They did help build this town though. And as to your second question, unfortunately, the great pyramids are a long way away, south of the Delta valley, actually." After Gabriel knocked the dust from his clothes, he said, "While we wait here for more information that will help us find Moses, let me get you up-to-date on how Joseph and later his Israelite brothers and their families came to Egypt. As I was telling you, Joseph came first and not by his own choice. You see, Joseph was the fair-haired favorite of his father Jacob – or Israel, his given name by God. All the other brothers tried to live up to Joseph's standards, but Israel was always saying to each of them 'why can't you do this like Joseph' or 'you should act more like Joseph' or 'Joseph always does it this way.' This really made his brothers furious and they grew to envy and hate him."

"Oh, I remember this story," Bethany said, excited to add to the conversation. "His father gave him this totally rad robe."

"Err ... you mean the so-called 'coat of many colors?'" Gabriel asked.

"Yeah, that's the one. And Joseph told his brothers about a dream he had where all of them would one day bow down to him, right?"

"Correct! You do know this story!" Gabriel continued, "Now, the sons of Israel were tending their sheep near the town of Shechem and further north in a town named Dothan, both in Canaan, when along comes Joseph, their seventeen-year-old brother, strolling around in his gorgeous coat that his father had given him. This was too much for his other brothers to stand, and they considered killing him. Fortunately, his brothers Reuben and Judah persuaded the others not to shed his blood, but to sell him to some traders who were passing by on their way from Syria to Egypt."

"Coach, isn't there a town called Dothan in Alabama?" she asked.

"Let me think. Yes, yes, there is," Gabriel concluded. "I wonder if it also has two wells."

"Two wells?" Bethany looked puzzled.

"Yes, Dothan means 'two wells.' You see, in this town there were two well-like pits. These pits were meant to capture water whenever it rained. We are told in Genesis 37:24 that, prior to his sale, Joseph was cast into a pit that contained no water."

"How awful!" Bethany shuddered as she spoke.

"Indeed! As you may recall, his brothers basically sold him into slavery, and the traders purchased him and took him to Egypt. But Joseph was fortunate to have God's blessing. In Egypt, he prospered and was put in charge of the house of his master. Later, he was recognized to have quite a talent for interpreting dreams and ultimately, at the age of thirty, he was employed by the Pharaoh himself to be the overseer of all the land of Egypt!"

"Oh, is this the good news, bad news, cow dream story?" Bethany inquired.

"I'm not certain what you mean," Gabriel responded with an inquiring look.

"You know, my dad tells it like this," Bethany went on. "Joseph tells the Pharaoh that he's heard his cow dream and he's got some good news and some bad news, and asks him which he wants to hear first. The Pharaoh says, 'Give me the bad news first.' So Joseph says 'OK, the bad news is those seven lean cows mean you've got a major famine coming up, and it's going to last seven years. All your crops and cows are going to die, and I mean it's major starvation time!' The Pharaoh's eyes roll back in his head and he looks like he's going to faint. But before he does Joseph says, 'The good news is, we got seven good years to prepare for it!'"

Gabriel paused before speaking. "I'd hate to hear your father's explanation of the Ten Commandments." Gabriel then continued, "Well, in any event, as your story suggested, Joseph's dream came true, and when the famine came it was dreadful. It spread not only into Egypt but also into Canaan, where Jacob was still living with his remaining sons. So Jacob sent his sons into Egypt because he heard the people there had grain to sell, although neither Jacob nor his sons realized that Joseph was the person responsible for its storage and sale. Now when Joseph's brothers got to Egypt, they bowed down to him, just as Joseph had once predicted, because Joseph then held a high official position in Egypt. In a way, Joseph was as powerful as the Pharaoh of Egypt himself!"

"Didn't his brothers recognize him?" asked Bethany.

"No, they didn't," Gabriel responded. "It had been years since they had seen each other, and Joseph was probably dressed quite differently since he was now living with the Egyptians. Joseph, on the other hand, recognized them almost immediately after they told him the name of their home town."

Bethany stood up and pointing her finger at Gabriel said, "Coach, I hope Joseph threw his brothers in jail to teach them a lesson... those, those scoundrels!"

Gabriel grinned, "Yes, they were scoundrels, weren't they? And Joseph played a great trick on them to make them reflect on what they had done to him. Why don't you read the story while I look for Moses? You can find it in Genesis, Chapters 42 through 45," he said as he handed her his Bible and left to look for Moses.

Upon Gabriel's return sometime later, he greeted Bethany but she did not answer. She continued to read with a smile on her face.

"This is really interesting stuff!" Bethany said excitedly, as she continued to read. "I mean I found the part that says that they brought Joseph's dad – you know, Israel – and his entire family to Goshen in Egypt so they would have food and wouldn't starve. And it says right here in Chapter 47, verse 11 that this land was just outside the city of Rameses, and that's where we are now! Right, Coach?"

"Young lady, you are reading ahead ... two chapters ahead to be precise. Watch out, you may spoil my surprise!"

"I'm sorry, Gabriel. It's just that I wanted to know what happened to Joseph and his brothers and whether Joseph really forgave them for what they did to him."

"His brothers were worried too," Gabriel responded, "but Joseph did forgive them since he realized that God had turned their evil into good. You see, he realized that his being in Egypt, interpreting that dream, and preparing for the famine had saved the lives of many people, including his own family. Anyway, Joseph lived in Goshen with his family quite happily for the rest of his life, and this is reported in the last chapter of Genesis, Chapter 50, that is."

"You mean that we've finished with Genesis and Moses wasn't mentioned even once?"

"That's right, so remember that even though the Law – that is, the first five books of the Bible – is often called the

Five Books of Moses, Moses doesn't get any 'press' until Exodus – the second book. But that's where he really gets to steal the show, so to speak. By the way, you still need to learn the first bookshelf."

"You mean the Law, History and Poetry?" Bethany asked. "That's hard. Will you help me?"

"Certainly! Let's write a silly poem to help you remember," Gabriel said. "It will probably take us about an hour to come up with one crazy enough to excite your macro-association brain cells."

Chapter 10
Genny's Sis Throws Ex-o-dust

Gabriel and Bethany worked hard to create a poem on the first twenty-two books of the Bible. Bethany decided that three verses would be best; one for the books of Law, one for the books of general History, and one for the books of Poetry. Bethany also had to think of a way to remember that three of the books had more than one volume. (Gabriel explained to her that those books were so long that they each had to be put on two scrolls, which is what the scribes of that period used for writing.) Fortunately, these books were conveniently all together which made it easier to remember. Bethany then carefully wrote down the final version of the poem on a piece of paper that Gabriel had provided. Bethany called it "Genny's Sis" for a take-off on "Genesis."

GENNY'S SIS

Law   *Genny's Sis* throws *Ex-o-dust,*   Genesis, Exodus
          While *Levi* teaches not *to cuss;*   Leviticus
          And *Numbers* gives us one plus three,   Numbers
          Which equals *Dude-or-Ron-or me.*   Deuteronomy

History	While *Joshua Judges Ruth,*	Joshua, Judges Ruth
	The trial *t[w]o Samuel* is reported;	1st & 2nd Samuel
	And *t[w]o* the *King's Chronicles*	1st & 2nd Kings
	To be recorded;	1st & 2nd Chronicles
	While on *Ezra's Knee* (*oh my! ah*),	Ezra, Nehemiah
	Pretty *Esther* is supported.	Esther
Poetry	*Job* thinks poetry's no laughing matter,	Job
	He opens *P[s]alms* to hear *Proverbs* chatter;	Psalms, Proverbs
	And sings *Ec-cles-i-as-tes* if you please;	Ecclesiastes
	Or if you think it nice,	
	A *Song of Solomon* will suffice.	Song of Solomon

"Magnificent!" complimented Gabriel. "Simply magnificent! That's so interesting even a nine-year-old could learn these books easily. Bravo, Bethany!"

Bethany smiled, "I made it as silly as possible, and I must say it has a 'Strange Saturday' feeling to it." (As she made this statement, she noticed that her doggie friend continued his exercises even without her participation. He had now developed a new game for himself. First he would jump up on a large rock with his bone in his mouth. Then, tossing the bone into the air, he would attempt to catch it with his teeth before it hit the ground. Sometimes he would also try to make his body flip in the air and then attempt to catch the bone, but found this to be a most difficult maneuver.)

"Strange Saturday? What is Strange Saturday?"

"It's this great children's book that my mom and dad always read to me before bedtime. You see, on Strange Saturday there was a boot in a vase that was completely out of place," Bethany said with a smile.

"What in the name of Joshua's Jericho are you talking about?" Gabriel inquired, looking perplexed.

"Oh, you know, the story where the little kid goes to his school and finds his teacher, Miss Poole, wearing a tutu and she has a hula hoop around her waist. And then he sees the four Stueban Brothers whose clothes are worn inside out. Didn't anybody ever read that book to you when you were young?"

Gabriel interjected, "I believe it was written well after my early years."

"Oh, oh, yes ... I guess you didn't have as many books back then."

"Young lady, have you ever heard of the printing press?"

"Of course, my dad says it was one of the greatest inventions in the world – ranks right up there with the wheel, steam engine, computer and mute button on the TV's remote control, he always says."

"Well, in my younger years, I never heard of it because it had yet to be invented. You might say my formal education started very late. I still love to read any good book I can get my hands on."

"You still read books?" Bethany asked, surprised.

"Of course, what do you think we angels do all day?" Gabriel said abruptly, somewhat offended by her inquiry.

"Golf?" she asked innocently. "At least that's what my Uncle Lot hopes."

"Why, may I ask, does your uncle hope that?"

"He told me once that the only way that he could ever hope to get into heaven is if God has a good sense of humor and likes golf. I don't really understand why, except that he keeps saying that the one thing he has done religiously throughout his life is attend the Church of the Holy Green each Sunday."

Gabriel was almost ready to respond to this statement when he suddenly raised his hands to his temple, as if he had a migraine headache. He then said, with his hands still touching his head, "Bethany, I'm getting a signal. I think I know where to find Moses." Gabriel then motioned for Bethany and Oba to stand beside him so that they might be transported to their new destination by the use of his travel gadget. But before they took off, she asked if they could go to their new destination by horseback. Within moments, the large white stallion appeared and whisked the three of them across the desert toward the Sinai peninsula, as Bethany gleamed with excitement at the most wondrous horseback ride ever.

Upon arriving at their new location, Gabriel commented, "We are in the Desert of Paran, just outside Kadesh-barnea. We must wait until tomorrow afternoon. Then it will be time to see Moses. In the meantime, I will prepare some dinner while I make sure you know how Moses and his people got here and answer any questions that you may have up to this point. Also, if time permits, you should read up on several areas that are important for our upcoming contest."

As they ate, they discussed: how Moses demanded that the Pharaoh let his people go; the plagues and Passover; how the Israelites escaped to the wilderness; and how Moses received the Ten Commandments at Mt. Sinai – many miles south of their present location.

After a while, Bethany said, "You know Coach, there're a couple of things that really bother me. Why didn't the Israelites go directly to Canaan instead of wandering around in the wilderness for forty years? And another thing, you said earlier that Moses' tribe, the Levites, didn't get any property. Why was that?"

"Bethany, your first question will be answered tomorrow. As to your property question, let me give you an overview. As you will recall, each of the families of the twelve sons of Jacob got specific territory in Canaan, with two exceptions. Here, let's look at a map," Gabriel went on, "to see how the property probably was divided, although some of the borders are not known with certainty." And with that he pulled out a map from his back pocket.

"Oh," Bethany responded, while reviewing the map. "I

see that Levi is missing, and where is Joseph's property? Surely he wasn't left out after all he did for God and his family."

"On the contrary, he was richly rewarded through his two sons, Manasseh and Ephraim. That is, Joseph's family got a double share!"

"Oh, yes. I see Manasseh's and Ephraim's property, along with the names of Joseph's other brothers. Hey, why is the name of Dan way up north while his property is along the coast, and why is Manasseh's property so large?" Bethany said, reviewing the map closely.

"Good questions! You know, it seems that for every answer I give, you have two more questions! As to Dan, look where his property is located – in the midst of the powerful Philistines! Dan's family tried to take the property but had problems overthrowing such a strong opponent and finally decided to go north and take the town of Laish for their own. They were successful and renamed the town 'Dan,' after their forefather. As to your question about the huge size of Manasseh's property, I'll have to think about that one. I really don't know the answer off the top of my halo. Let's see, Manasseh was Jacob's grandson. Possibly it was because Manasseh was also Joseph's oldest son, so he was the oldest son of the oldest son of the marriage of Jacob and Rachel." After a brief pause, Gabriel continued, "Now, let's move on to your inquiry about the Levites. Moses and his brother, Aaron, were Levites, and Aaron's job was to perform priestly functions, such as making offerings to God on behalf of all the tribes."

"You mean they were like our ministers?

"In a way, yes. They were 'devoted' – that is, set apart as belonging to God – to take care of the worship rituals, making sure that the offering ceremonies were properly performed, and so forth. This was most appropriate I think in that it was Moses who brought the Ten Commandments from Mount Sinai, and his family was the first caretaker of God's holy word. Now, do you know where these tablets were placed?"

"Give me a hint, Coach," Bethany pleaded.

"The Ark of ..." Gabriel complied.

"I know, I know, the Ark of the Covenant! Right?"

"Correct! See, you have learned something in Sunday school!" Gabriel said hoping to bolster her confidence.

"Oh, no! I learned that when I saw the old movie 'Raiders of the Lost Ark.'"

Gabriel looked disappointed and then upon reflection responded, "Oh well, at least there are some good religious movies being produced. The Ten Commandments, with

Charlton Heston, was one of my favorites. And The Prince of Egypt was another."

"Well, it wasn't really a religious … you see, Indiana Jones was an archaeologist that …," then realizing, as she looked into Gabriel's heavenly blue eyes, that to go on would only disappoint him more, she stopped her sentence short. Changing the subject, she went on, "You know, it makes some sense to me that God wouldn't let Levi's family have property 'cause with property you can borrow money."

"I don't understand."

"Well, my Uncle Lot always says the worst thing that can happen to a minister is if he gets his hands on a lot of property since the first thing he's going to do with it is use it to borrow some money to buy time on some television station. Then he's going to ask people for money so that he can buy more property – hospitals, schools, resort areas, stuff like that – and use that property to borrow more money to buy more time on TV. My uncle says this could nibble away at the major networks' audience for those mindless 'sitcoms' and, along with the erosion of audiences generally caused by the explosion in cable and satellite TV, the major networks won't be able to sell their advertisement for as much. And you know what will happen then!"

"I do? I mean, no, I don't! What, pray tell, will happen?" Gabriel said in anticipation.

"Foreigners will come in and buy these network stations dirt cheap and make further progress in controlling our entertainment industry!"

"Is that bad?"

"It could be. According to my uncle, we could end up with our entire movie and television entertainment limited to King Kong, Godzilla and Kung Fu films, along with a hundred versions of the Gospel Hour."

Gabriel shook his head in amazement and then

considered how much they had to cover before the contest and mused whether Bethany would really be ready.

Later that evening Gabriel told Bethany many stories regarding the Levites and of the laws regarding the proper form of worship and answered a host of Bethany's other questions. As usual, Oba stayed close to Bethany's side, since she would often stroke his soft fur as she talked. Gabriel even told her briefly about the Levites' rights to control forty-eight cities throughout the family's properties, including the six "sanctuary" cities, although careful not to open the conversation to any extraneous words of wisdom quoted from Uncle Lot. Bethany and Gabriel talked well into the night as they camped beneath the brilliant starlit sky, with only a small fire to dim the Almighty's celestial lamps above. All was quiet as they finally fell asleep.

A few hours later, Bethany was awakened by the howl of a wolf in the far distance. When she opened her eyes, her mind began to spin as she viewed the vast heavenly bodies above her head. For the next hour, she pondered her situation, reflecting on what the next day of her life would bring and whether she would be successful in her task. Unable to sleep, she rolled to one side of her sleeping bag and spotted next to her the JOY gadget which had been left on by Gabriel. Tiny red and blue lights were blinking, enticing her with every blink to pick it up and scrutinize the device more closely. Apparently, Gabriel, who continued to sleep soundly, had failed to put it away before falling asleep. Bethany hesitated but could not stand the temptation; she reached over and picked it up to observe how it might work. It had a large dial in the center surrounded by an array of buttons and a small display screen at the top. As she sat up, she examined it closely. Turning it around to view the backside, the gizmo slipped from her hand. As it began to fall, she attempted to grab it with her other hand, and her fingers inadvertently hit several buttons before catching it securely. Suddenly, she felt strange. In an instant, she was "zapped" away into the night!!

Chapter 11
A Nasty, Nasty Cut

Bethany observed her new surroundings. She was inside what appeared to be a hospital room. "Why did the time machine take me here?" she thought to herself. It was a frightening sight to behold: In the corner of the room was a light blue curtain half drawn around the bed with tubes running everywhere and a heart monitor beeping every few seconds – confirming the frailty of the patient's condition. Bethany leaned her head to one side to try to get a better look at what was behind the curtain. She could only see the back of the head of the patient in the bed, but she guessed it was female by her rather long hair. She again wondered why she was there, as she heard faint voices of a man and woman talking behind the curtain. The woman began to weep. Bethany strained to hear their conversation. As she decided to move a few steps closer, the woman got up to get a tissue passing by the curtain long enough for Bethany to catch a glimpse of her face. Bethany was shocked! It was her mother! And next to her was her father! Bethany thought that something must have happened to her sister Genny, but what? She dashed around the curtain and saw the unthinkable – the patient was not Genny. It was her! Horrified and confused, Bethany wondered how this could have happened. She tried to get her parents' attention, but the shock of her situation and her time travel caused her to be speechless. In her head she was yelling, "I'm okay. Mom. Dad. I'm fine. Why can't you hear me? And why can't you see me?" Realizing that trying to communicate with them was useless, she just gazed at her parents in disbelief.

"How's she doing today?" said a gruff voice that Bethany recognized in an instant as her Uncle Lot.

"About the same, Lot," Mrs. Clarke answered. "It's sweet that you came by again. Listen, Bob and I have been talking, and we really appreciate your visits, but you really don't have to do so much. I mean, you've been coming by every day and staying for three or four hours. We don't want you to feel that you've got to do that. We'll be fine and, of course, we'll call you if there is any change in her condition." (Bethany was surprised that Uncle Lot had been by to see about her every day. Tears came to her eyes when she remembered the last words she had said to him. She was so confused.)

"I don't mind at all. It's given me time to catch up on things going on with the family. Listen, I've got to run an errand or two. Can I get you anything while I'm out?"

"No, Lot. We're just fine. Thanks though," Mrs. Clarke responded.

"OK. I'll be back later."

After Lot left, Mr. and Mrs. Clarke next sat down on the bed and began to hold each of Bethany's hands in theirs. Her parents' eyes stared blankly toward Bethany's face, unable to focus due to lack of sleep. "Oh, this is all my fault," her father commented quietly. "I should have never let her cut through that park alone. I should have gone with her. Then none of this would have happened. I'm so sorry,

Bethany. Please forgive me," he said as he squeezed her hand tightly.

Mrs. Clarke responded, "Bob, this was not your fault, so don't go blaming yourself. It was an accident. You can't follow Bethany everywhere and protect her from any harm." Bethany nodded in agreement, wishing she could put her arms around her dad and take away the pain and guilt he was feeling. If only she had listened to him and stayed on the path, this would have never happened, she thought. Momentarily, a doctor entered the room.

"Good morning," Dr. Williams said as he approached the bed with a slight smile. "Any new developments last night?" (Dr. Williams was in his early fifties, but his boyish blond hair made him look much younger.)

"No, not really," Mr. Clarke said, trying to compose himself, "although Nancy said she thought she noticed some facial movement around 2:00 p.m."

"I don't know, Dr. Williams," Mrs. Clarke added, "it might have been my eyes playing a trick on me, but I thought I saw a faint smile on Bethany's face. It appeared that she was having a pleasant dream or something. Is that possible?"

"People in a comatose state do sometimes dream," Dr. Williams responded. "Let's take a look at our little patient."

As he examined her eyes under their closed lids, Dr. Williams went on, "A nasty, nasty cut and blow on the back of her head. It must have been a large, sharp rock that she hit when she rolled down that hill. It's a miracle that she's alive. She lost a lot of blood."

"Doctor, it's been five days now and she's still in a coma," Mrs. Clarke interjected with great concern and frustration in her voice. "Isn't there anything else we can do?"

"Mrs. Clarke," Dr. Williams responded, "I can appreciate your concern, but despite the fact that Northview Hospital has one of the best trauma centers in the city, in these situations there's not much we can do but wait. Her condition has stabilized a great deal. Remember, five days ago I thought she had less than a thirty percent chance of pulling through; now, I think it's close to fifty-fifty. If Mr. Clarke had found Bethany just fifteen minutes later, we wouldn't be having this conversation today. She's alive. Let's hold on to that for right now."

"You know," Mr. Clarke said, reflecting on the day of the accident, "it's strange how her uncle just happened to be pulling up in our drive and heard a faint yell come from the park. I was inside and didn't hear a thing. Lot rarely comes over to visit unannounced, but Bethany had left her Bible at his house at lunch, and, for some reason, he thought it was important to bring it to her right away. And am I ever glad he did. We were both pretty shaken up when we found her bleeding and unconscious in the woods."

Dr. Williams finished his examination, and then turned to the couple after a moment of reflection, "You know there is one other thing you could do."

"What's that?" Mrs. Clarke eagerly inquired.

"Pray," he said. "Your whole family is going to need all the strength and help you can get in dealing with this one." With this closing comment, Dr. Williams departed to visit his next patient.

After Dr. Williams left them alone and disappeared past the end of the hall, Mrs. Clarke piped up, "You know, Bob, over the past five days I've had time to think about a lot of things, including what I viewed as all the major problems in my life. Now they all seem rather trivial. All the things that I thought we really needed – that new car, that addition to the house and that vacation in the Bahamas – really aren't that important now. Maybe they never should have been. What I don't understand though, what I really don't understand is why ... why is this happening to us? Why, why on earth is this happening to Bethany!" Mrs. Clarke's voice began to crack as she wrenched her handkerchief tightly with her hands. "She's just a little girl!" she choked as tears appeared in the corners of her eyes. (Bethany wanted to comfort her mom, as she absorbed the situation and realized that this seemed much too real to be a dream, although she didn't want to admit it to herself.)

Mr. Clarke reached for his wife's hand, and sat quietly for a moment trying to come to grips with his own emotions before responding. "I know, I know," he said almost in a whisper. "All I need – all I want is three healthy kids again." He closed his eyes and said in a much louder voice, as they held hands, "Good God, just give us back Bethany! She's got so much more to give to this world!" his emotions finally seeping out, trying as he did to restrain them.

Bethany sat by attentively as Mr. and Mrs. Clarke continued to discuss many things, including whether they should tell Stopher and Genny the real situation – that their sister may never recover but could remain in a coma and ultimately die. They were certain that the question would come up soon and wanted to make sure they were in agreement on their response. As they talked, they shared those special moments they each had with Bethany: The birthdays, the Christmases, the school plays, the quiet talks before bedtime, all gave meaning to their lives and were memories that would live forever in their hearts. Even though it made them sad, Bob and Nancy felt better in reliving those memories, and they once again prepared themselves for the uncertainty that waited ahead.

Bethany, not able to stand the sight any longer of her family in such pain over her condition, returned her thoughts to the JOY device. As tears came to her eyes, she, mostly out of despair, pushed a button on the travel machine which looked a bit like a "redial" function on a phone. Almost instantaneously she was "zapped" away –

miraculously back to the place in Egypt where Gabriel and Bethany had made camp.

*   *   *   *   *   *   *

Everything in the camp was just as she had left it, except Gabriel was now awake, pacing around. As she moved toward Gabriel, he continued to walk around, his anger growing with each step he took. "I know where you have been, young lady. You should have never used JOY to travel in time. How could you!! I specifically told you not to! You may have altered all of history with your foolish curiosity traveling without clearance!! I should have never let it out of my sight. God's very, very upset with me about this!"

Bethany began to weep, realizing the possible consequences of her actions. "I'm sorry, Gabriel. I'm so, so sorry! What's going to happen to me? And what is going to happen to you? I'm so confused right now," she sobbed, as she began to fidget and walk about holding her head down in quiet reflection.

Gabriel then realized the fear she was experiencing due to her observations in the hospital. As his heart melted seeing her in such pain, he opened his arms to her and pulled her close. "All I know is that God has a long-range plan for both of us, even though we don't always know what it is. And the Lord will be with us and guide us if we only ask. You know, God has a plan for just about everything. Sometimes humans just can't see it or figure it out. It's a bit like the bumblebee: Based on its weight and wing area, some scientists have calculated that it shouldn't be able to fly – not enough 'lift.' God's design provides that lift, and we just have to trust in that and not worry." As Gabriel gave her a handkerchief to dry her eyes, he continued, "Right now, you are needed to complete one of three tasks that God has chosen for you to perform. Rest up today and gather your strength. Tomorrow I will tell you more."

Chapter 12
Ammonites, Moabites, Edomites
and Midianites – AMEM!

The next morning Bethany awoke refreshed, cooled by the desert night air. Gabriel had been up an hour earlier and was ready to serve her and her floppy-eared friend, Oba, a quick breakfast, which they hurriedly ate, for Gabriel was anxious to resume their studies. Among other passages, Gabriel had her read Numbers 13:1-25 which described Moses sending a representative from each tribe into the Promised Land of Canaan to find out about those that dwelled there. As usual, Bethany read much more than Gabriel had requested. Gabriel then disappeared for almost thirty minutes during which time Bethany decided to continue to work with her canine athlete on his high jumps. With his uncanny balance and jumping ability, Oba learned to leap from the ground to Bethany's shoulder while she walked about. Upon Gabriel's return, Bethany had a number of questions for him to address.

"Coach, going to spy on the people in Canaan must have been pretty exciting," Bethany started her conversation. "I mean there wasn't just the Canaanites to watch out for, but there were all these other people who lived in the area. You know, it's very confusing trying to determine where everybody lived. For example, Numbers 13:29 says the Amalekites lived in the Negeb and Moses

said go into the Negeb, but where is the Negeb? Are we near there? And then the Israelite spies were supposed to go to the hill country. Where is that? I mean, you may have told me before, but I just can't remember."

Gabriel smiled. "Possibly a map would help. It does get a little complex." Gabriel then pulled from his back pocket some paper and quickly sketched out a map for Bethany to study and showed it to her.

"Now that's most of those who lived in the region," Gabriel said, looking relatively satisfied. "I also listed several major cities. Remember, the Promised Land is generally referred to as stretching north to south from the towns of Dan to Beersheba. Other important towns, especially after the united kingdom of Israel split into two parts, were the capital cities of Shechem and, later on, Samaria, both in the North, and Jerusalem in the South. We'll talk about the northern and southern kingdoms later." Then pointing to places on the map, Gabriel continued, "Mount Nebo, which we visited earlier, is where Moses viewed the Promised Land, and, of course, Jericho is where Joshua fought his famous battle shortly after the Israelites entered Canaan."

"Oh, is this the same Joshua that was one of the spies who originally checked out the Promised Land?"

"None other," answered Gabriel. "And I believe it was Joshua's bravery that made God decide to appoint him as the successor to lead the Israelites after Moses' death. You will learn more about Joshua shortly."

Bethany, after reviewing the map for a moment, bit her lip and shook her head. "I still think it's confusing," she said.

"AMEM!" Gabriel said with enthusiasm.

"You mean Amen, don't you?" Bethany questioned.

"No, I mean AMEM," Gabriel answered. "You see, it's a memory aid I use to remember those people who lived on the east side of the Jordan River. North to south or top to bottom: the Ammonites, the Moabites, the Edomites and the Midianites. On the other hand, the Canaanites lived mostly on the west side of the Jordan River."

"Wow! Along with the Israelites that's a lot of 'ites.' What does that word ending mean anyway?" she inquired.

"Generally, it means 'people of' so that, for example, Israelites and Moabites means the people of Israel and Moab," Gabriel responded quickly.

Bethany cocked her head to one side and smiled as she thought about what Gabriel had just said. "Oxymoron! Oxymoron!" she shouted with a twinkle in her eye.

"What are you talking about?"

"I just though of an oxymoron – the word termite; it doesn't make any sense – 'the people of term' – get real!"

Gabriel smiled and then burst into laughter as he realized her problem. "Child, you're doing it! Macro-association! Bless you! We're going to be ready for that contest. I can tell. However, I must be more careful how I explain things to you. You see, the root meaning of 'ite' literally means 'inhabitants' or 'those who dwell within' and 'term' comes from the Latin word 'termes' meaning 'wood'. So you see, my special angel, termite is not really an oxymoron. Those who dwell in the wood should be called termites. It does make sense."

"Hey, you called me an angel. I'm not an angel! You're the angel, remember?!

"I'm sorry. Totally a slip of the tongue, I assure you. But there are worse things that could happen to you than coming to live with us angels."

"I guess you're right, but I really get frightened when I think about the 'Big D' word," Bethany said as she shivered.

"What 'Big D' word?"

"You know – Death," she responded.

Gabriel turned away from Bethany. As he looked towards the sky, he spoke quietly, "Please Lord, I don't know where she's going with this, but give me wisdom to comfort her."

"You know, I've always wondered why God lets little children die."

Gabriel reflected for a moment, still wondering whether he should try to change the subject or respond directly to her question. After a long silence, Gabriel said, "Bethany that's a difficult question – a question I have asked myself many times. I have seen so many children on earth die due to lack of proper food, clothing and medical care. Of course, all people have to go some day to make room for their children and their children's children. That shouldn't scare you. Oh, I know I told you there's a lot of hard work in heaven. But it's really mostly fun for people – different assignments virtually every week, meeting new friends and lots of travel."

"You mean it's like the Army?"

"No! No! Take my word for it. It's quite different from the Army," Gabriel went on. "Anyway, back to your 'children' question. I'll tell you what I think, but you must understand that this is something I haven't personally discussed with God. It's just my view. OK?"

"I guess so."

"OK. Now, I think ... no ... no ... I *know* how powerful God is. The Lord can perform multiple miracles simultaneously if the Almighty so desires. God made not only our earth, but also our solar system and the universe. To the extent that we don't mess things up with our pollution and wars, God keeps things running pretty smoothly, I think you would agree. But the universe is so big! Bethany, have you ever thought about how really huge the universe is? Take the Milky Way, which is made up of distant stars in our own galaxy. There are well over 100 billion stars in the Milky Way, which is over 100,000 light years across! And there are lots of galaxies that are larger!"

"Wow! 100 billion stars just in our galaxy! That's huge!"

"Yes that is. And the universe is very complicated. For example, did you know that each day neutrinos – small particles with little or no mass traveling at the speed of light from the sun – pass through your body at the rate of trillions per second. Yet, they apparently don't harm you," Gabriel then folded his arms and waited for a response.

"Gee, that sounds like what my mom does every night before she puts me to bed, and I hate it!"

"Hate what?"

"Getting bombarded with her kisses. She says it won't hurt me, but I hate getting ... getting ... neutrinosed with kisses!"

Gabriel, somewhat taken aback by Bethany's response, let her comment sink in and then began to smile. "Neutrinosed! Neutrinosed! What a great saying. I love it!" After a short pause, Gabriel began again. "As I was saying, this universe is complicated, very complicated. Why, did you know that on the earth alone there are estimated to be between two to four million different species of insects?"

"The earth alone?" Bethany said, picking up on Gabriel's use of the word 'alone.' "Do you mean that there are insects or other forms of life on places other than the earth?" Bethany's eyes got as big as sand dollars as she awaited Gabriel's answer.

Gabriel, realizing he had opened another Pandora's box, responded by saying, "Now, Bethany, you must realize that I'm basically an earth angel. I'm either in heaven or here on earth. You know, it's a big universe out there and there's a lot I don't know." Looking at the sky, he stood still for a long pause and then continued. "I will tell you this though," he said with a gleam in his eye, "God's out of town a good bit, and I think he must be on business!" Gabriel then turned and made eye contact with Bethany before further addressing her inquiry. "Now getting back to your question, as you can see, this world is very, very complex. I can't imagine how God keeps everything going as smoothly as it does. I finally concluded that there were things about the Lord's plan that we'll never be able to understand fully. We've just got to accept that, although it's hard to do."

"Gabriel, how do you think God finds out about problems?"

"Well, remember God often works through people and, of course, us angels. The Lord might hear someone calling out for help through a prayer or something or an angel might bring a matter to God's attention."

"When lots of people pray for the same thing to happen is God more likely to answer that prayer?"

"No, I don't think so. To God a single voice is as important as many. But I think our Creator is more likely to hear the message right away if it's coming from more than one source. Therefore, if the prayer's one that should be answered in the fashion requested, God's in a better position to react more quickly. And, I'll tell you another thing, God's a wonderful champion for children. They have great faith, and God knows that. They also do many foolish things growing up. And God knows that, too. So the Almighty made their bodies to bend more without breaking and to heal more quickly than do the bodies of adults. But I think that sometimes God gets there too late to help or determines, for some reason that I really can't explain, that it would be better for this little boy or girl to join us angels in heaven. It's really rough on the family that's left behind, but, believe me, kids love heaven. You just have to trust God and have faith that the little ones will get especially good treatment in heaven. Does that answer your question?"

"Yes, I think it does, but I do have two other questions. Are there many fun things for children to do in heaven, and is God a man or a woman?" Bethany inquired.

Gabriel paused before speaking, "You know, Bethany,

you should definitely be in charge of a TV game show for a major network. You'd never be at a loss for questions for your contestants!" Gabriel then walked away from Bethany in deep thought, on occasion mumbling to himself as if he were trying to decide what to do or say next. Bethany was becoming a little anxious with the distance he was placing between himself and her. She was about to follow him when he finally turned and began walking back toward her, smiling and shaking his head. "I'll take the harder question first," Gabriel finally responded. "You know," he said pointing his finger at her, "in my early years I always thought God was a male. I mean, it seemed so logical viewing the people on earth. You see, I was familiar with the story of Adam and Eve, and males pretty much dominated the earth's political and social environment. So to believe that God was a female when men were generally running everything, didn't make much sense to me."

"Uncle Lot agrees with that a hundred percent. He says God made the world out of chaos and that shows that God is orderly and logical, just like a man. He says the Bible is clear that God made Adam first and then Eve and that man was made in God's image. Anyway, my uncle says the Bible's full of references to God using the pronoun 'He' so that there can't be any question on the point. But my mom tells him that he's flat wrong."

"Oh?" Gabriel said with an amused look on his face.

"Yes, she says that there are references in the Bible to God being a 'mother' figure and that women are much closer to God's true likeness. You see, she says that God made all these animals and that man was supposed to be different, with a much bigger brain so that he could reason and tell the difference from right and wrong and all that stuff. And then God made Adam, but his brain was not quite big enough. It was God's first attempt at making humans, you know."

"Yes, go on." Gabriel said encouragingly. "This sounds like it may be an interesting theory that I have not heard before."

"Well, anyway, God really liked Adam, although he was a little short on brainpower, so God decided to give him a helper who would be able to get him through the tough problems in life, and, of course, that was Eve. Mom says it was a little like the difference in the original Apple computer and its later upgrades – made by the same company, but lots more memory."

"How interesting," Gabriel said. "I'm curious, speaking of apples, what is your mom's view on why Eve ate from the so-called forbidden fruit and the whole 'original sin' theory?"

"Oh, she thinks she's got that figured out, too. What happened there was that Eve had been instructed by God not to tell Adam that she got the bigger brain and, of course, knew a lot more than he did. You see, the tree of knowledge represents Eve's brain. And, when she bit into that apple, that's symbolic of her sin in telling Adam the truth; she didn't see why it was such a big deal. But God knew that if Adam found out he had a smaller brain, he and Eve might not get along, since in the animal kingdom, where brains are not too important, the male is always in charge. So Adam would look around and think he was an oddball or something. Anyway, God punished Eve by making her a servant of Adam. After Eve died, the men thought all women were supposed to act like Eve, and it has taken thousands of years for women to convince men that they're not supposed to be the servant – it was only Eve's punishment, not theirs!"

"Fascinating. Truly, truly, fascinating! What does your uncle say to all this?"

"He just says, 'Women. Who can figure them!'" After a moment of silence, Bethany pushed forward with her inquiry, "Who is right, Gabriel? Mom or Uncle Lot?"

Gabriel cleared his throat as if he were about to make a great announcement, "I must say, I was surprised at what I found out in heaven about God."

"I knew it! I knew it!" Bethany exclaimed, "God's a She! Isn't He ... I mean She?"

Gabriel chuckled, and smiled, before responding, as he shook his head. "No She isn't!"

"Oh," Bethany said disappointedly. She then looked forward with a rather blank stare as she thought about what Gabriel had said. After a couple moments of deep thought, she responded "Wait a minute. She's not a She? That doesn't make sense!"

"Right. And She's not a He," Gabriel responded.

"You mean She's ... I mean God's an It?" Bethany commented in disbelief.

"Not exactly. You see, you might say that God is all three: He, She and It. Yet, God is neither human nor animal. God is God. The Lord is unique. While I try not to refer to God as a pronoun, it slips out sometimes, and the pronouns I use are 'He' or 'Him' since that's what makes me most comfortable. Now that I think about it, most of the times when God has communicated with humans the voice probably has been thought to be male, since that's what most people expect. And the writers of the Bible certainly lean in that direction. On the other hand, I must say your mother is correct that there are a number of maternal or mother-like qualities attributed to God in several books of the Bible, such as Isaiah and Psalms, and throughout the Song of Solomon. Anyway, since humans are capable of deep reasoning and moral behavior, they are more closely made to the likeness of God than are animals. In heaven, however, when God speaks to me, half the time, I can't tell whether the voice sounds more male or female. I guess it's natural that people will try to pigeonhole God as one sex or the other, although it's really a little silly. Don't ever try to put God in a box. The Almighty and Everlasting is much too big and will never fit!"

"Have you ever seen God?"

"Nope. But as I mentioned to you before, I talk – through prayer – with the Lord at least several times a day. God's my boss and my friend!" Having addressed the issue rather thoroughly, Gabriel next turned to Bethany's other question. "Now about your inquiry on whether there are any fun things to do in heaven, let me just say that there are thousands and give you one example. Remember the horseback ride we took to get here?"

"Oh yes. That was wonderful!" Bethany responded.

"Well, that's our equivalent to your merry-go-round ride back on earth," Gabriel said with a broad grin covering his face.

"No kidding!"

"Yep," said Gabriel. With his arms folded, Gabriel kicked the sand beneath his feet and then looked toward the sky, observing the position of the sun. "Hey, we've still got a while 'til Moses will be here. How would you like to take a little side trip 'back to the future' with me to the holy city of Jerusalem to see the Temple? It didn't exist at this point in time, you know. We can't stay too long, but it should prove educational and help you in your studies for the contest."

"Well, sure I'd love to go," Bethany responded. "Back to the future . . . Wow! How far back to the future are we going? I get very confused on the periods of time that are covered by the Old Testament. I mean who lived when, when the Temple was built and all that stuff."

"Stand beside me and when we get to the Temple, I'll give you the macro view," Gabriel said, as he pulled Bethany and her four-legged companion close to his side, and with an adjustment to his travel device, they disappeared in a flash.

Chapter 13
Dominoes of Life

Bethany rubbed her eyes as she realized that she was viewing the great Temple of Jerusalem. It was a rectangular-shaped stone building with small windows on the side. Two thirty-foot-tall bronze pillars marked the entrance. On top of each pillar sat an elaborately carved capital over eight feet in height. To the right of the Temple was a large altar. To the left was a hefty monument almost as large as the altar but for which Bethany could determine no purpose. There was a great deal of activity around the Temple, with people talking with what appeared to be priests, while merchants were selling their goods.

Bethany observed the sights and sounds outside the Temple with confusion and surprise. It was so loud, with men almost shouting over the commotion made by the many sheep, goats and cattle in the area. Doves and pigeons flew everywhere, as hundreds of other such birds were contained in large wooden boxes. (It reminded her of the crates of chickens loaded on the back of a large truck she had seen when her family traveled down the interstate on a weekend trip a few months before.) As a breeze suddenly turned in Bethany's direction, a sickening odor hit her nostrils. "Gabriel, what's that terrible smell?!!" Bethany inquired, as she wrinkled her nose so as to reduce the magnitude of the pungent stink overwhelming her.

"Animal sacrifices probably."

"Animal sacrifices?"

"Sure," Gabriel went on. "You see that little fellow over there wearing that bright outfit?"

Bethany closely focused on the little man. He wore a purple outer robe that looked like it was embroidered on the bottom in an alternating pattern of bells and some type of small fruit. On top of his robe was a golden orange apron that came slightly below his hips and was tied at the waist. Over the apron, he wore a breastplate, with four rows of square jewels of different colors. A blue linen turban with a rim of gold covered his head. Viewing how the little man carried himself with such showmanship and splendor, Bethany finally responded, "How could I not see him? Dressed like that, most rock stars' outfits would look boring! He's like the most excellent Mr. Hollywood! Who is he anyway?"

"The chief priest. He is in charge of the animal sacrifices, the last of which, best I can tell, was about an hour ago; probably a lamb or goat, I imagine."

"What! He slaughtered a little lamb! Shame on him!"

"No! No! He didn't slaughter it! He sacrificed it! There's a big difference, you know. You see, sacrifices were brought as gifts to God. The sacrifice offerings could only be performed by a priest at the altar of God. The animals sacrificed had to be males, except for birds. The most important part of the sacrifice was the way the blood of the animals was applied on the altar – it had to be dashed or smeared just so. Any old way wouldn't do. Would you like to go closer to the altar?"

"Oh! No! How barbaric!" Bethany exclaimed. "I mean,

I knew about these sacrifices, but it's different when you're here and can see and smell what's happening."

"It's better than the Canaanite practice of human sacrifices. Is it not?"

"Well, of course it is, Gabriel, but couldn't they use fruit or vegetables or something like that?"

"They did. Wheat, barley, olive oil, and frankincense were often used, along with even wine, I understand. But animals were sacrificed for special matters and on special occasions. Besides, without animals as part of the ritual, the English language could be without a very interesting word."

"What word?"

"The word 'scapegoat.' Do you know what that word means?"

"Sure. It's like when you're babysitting for your little sister and she breaks one of your mom's favorite dishes, while your mom's down the street having coffee with a neighbor. Anyway, when Mom gets back and finds out, instead of blaming the little brat that broke it, your mom blames you! Moms are weird like that sometimes. Anyway, that's a scapegoat, I think."

"Not bad, Bethany! And that transferring blame or guilt for the sins of another started at least as far back as the Israelites thousands of years ago. You see, God told Moses that on the Day of Atonement or 'Yom Kippur,' his brother, Aaron, was to take a live goat inside the Temple. This is the one day of the year that the priests could help the Israelites, collectively, as a nation of people, repair any wrongdoing and get 'right' with God. Then, Aaron was to sprinkle some blood of a bull and of a goat on the Ark of the Covenant and to ask God to forgive the sins of the Israelites. In a way, God was asked to purify all the Israelites – you know, make them clean and pure. After that, Aaron was to place his hands on the head of the goat and thereby transfer the people's sins to it and then allow it to 'escape' into the wilderness, taking the people's sins with it. And that's where the word scapegoat comes from – 'escape' plus 'goat.' Get it!"

"I don't believe it. Really?"

"Yep. If you don't believe me, you can read about it in Leviticus, Chapter 16, verses 8 through 22."

"You know, Coach, maybe my mom would let me get a billy goat. He could come in handy, couldn't he?"

Gabriel smiled and shook his finger at her. "Now, Bethany, you're not a priest, are you?"

"Guess not. Forget the goat," Bethany responded. "Hey, how 'bout I take home Oba? He'd be a great pet!" Bethany exclaimed, as her "best friend" in the animal world began to romp around, circling and charging her in a playful fashion. Finally, as she clapped her hands twice, the chocolate-colored dog jumped into Bethany's open arms and received the warm hug that he enjoyed greatly.

"Bethany, that's not likely going to happen. At some point, we've got to find his owner who probably misses him more than you can imagine." Gabriel then motioned to Bethany to follow him up the stairs into the Temple complex. It was quiet and deserted inside. The interior was exquisite. The floors and walls were wood overlaid with gold and the walls glistened with carvings of flowers, palm trees and cherubim – the second order angels known for their great knowledge. (To the people in this region, palm trees were popular since, in a land surrounded by deserts, the palm symbolized life – for where there is a palm, there must be a source of water to make it grow.) There were a number of gold lampstands throughout the room and a small incense altar, again made of wood and overlaid with gold.

"Gabriel, this place is beautiful!" Bethany said in an excited whisper. "But why aren't there any people in here worshiping?"

"Bethany, the worshiping was done mostly out in the Temple courtyard area by the altar, as part of the sacrifice offerings of fruit and animals. The Temple was so holy that only certain priests were allowed to enter, primarily to maintain it as God's private residence, you might say. Notice on the outside that it looks more like a fort than a house of worship, and that's for a reason. The Temple is basically divided into three main parts, back to front, with storerooms on the sides. You just passed through the porch area, and we are now in the middle room. The storerooms are filled with gold and other precious metals, religious objects and valuable gifts given to God by the Hebrew people. So you see, its fort-like structure has a purpose – to protect the 'booty,' so to speak."

"What's back there in the last room?" Bethany, still whispering, asked.

"Oh, that's the inner sanctuary or the 'Holy of Holies' as it is sometimes called. That's where they keep the Ark of the Covenant! You know, where they keep the Ten Commandments!" Gabriel said raising his voice slightly for emphasis. "Only the high priest could go in that area and only on one day of the year – the Day of Atonement. Remember?" Bethany nodded. "Now, Bethany, sit down. I want to talk with you about people and dates in the Old Testament. For the contest, you won't have to know exact dates, but you will be asked questions that will require you to have some knowledge of when people lived and when things happened, within a hundred years or so. That seems reasonable, doesn't it?"

"Why, I don't know. I mean the Old Testament covers thousands of years and there's so many events and people … I just don't know how I could ever be expected to remember them. And anyway, why are dates and these old people so important? I mean, who cares when these people lived or what year things happened in? It was so long ago."

Gabriel thought for a moment and then responded. "Let me address your second question first. Exact dates generally aren't that important. In fact, sometimes we don't know exact dates. But it is important to have a general feeling for the time in which things happen and an understanding of the order of things. For example, do you think it's important to know whether George Washington crossed the Delaware before Abe Lincoln gave the Gettysburg address?"

"Oh yeah, that's pretty basic. George Washington was our founding father who helped establish America. And Abe Lincoln, well, he helped save the union of our country."

"Right. You might say that Washington helped set up your 'laws of freedom' and Lincoln helped secure them. This is similar to the relationship of Moses, who gave us God's laws, and Nehemiah, a later governor of Judah, who helped maintain them. And thinking that Lincoln came before Washington would seem illogical since you know the relationship of how Lincoln held onto the growth of your country which Washington had helped form. It's that connectivity of time and people that gives us a sense of understanding of how all of us are affected by – and often owe a debt of gratitude to – others who came before us. You might call it the dominoes of life. Each life touches the next and, if the dominoes are properly placed and set in motion, a beautiful pattern is formed by that connectivity. If too large a gap in our dominoes is left, then that connectivity may be lost."

"The dominoes of life – that's really deep."

"I'm glad you like it. Anyway, Abraham and his descendants were chosen to help other people begin to develop a close relationship with God. And the dominoes of Abraham and his family – that early journey – are reflected in the Old Testament. Of course, that connectivity is continued in the New Testament with the birth and life of God's son, Jesus Christ. God wants us to see the whole story – that beautiful domino pattern."

"Oh, you mean it's like family history and which great

granddaddy did what to help his son do this, so that today we have this family land dating back hundreds of years. OK, I see your point. I'll try to learn some dates! But I still don't know how I'll ever remember all of them."

"Bear with me. That's why you have such an outstanding teacher – to teach you ways to remember the important events and dates. OK? Now, can you remember seven dates and seven people? And the events associated with those dates and people? You know, kind of a 'Super Seven' list."

"Of course I can. I'm not a ..."

"A doofus?" Gabriel responded before Bethany could finish. "Boy, that's a great word!" he went on, with a silly smile on his face. I know you're not, but this memory game will test your wits as well as your memory! Remember how I told you that you would have to stand three trials while you were in the past? This is your first. You must open the three gates, each of which leads closer to where you wish to be and which is in the order of their history. You will meet one named "Old Woman I Know" who will help you with your quest."

"Gabriel, who is this woman?"

"Oh, she is a very special person *and* the relative of a very significant person. Treat her with respect. She is very wise and always speaks the truth. However, she acts a bit strangely and suffers from spooner-sylloquatia."

"Spooner what?"

"Spooner-sylloquatia; it's, well ... you'll see. Just hang in there – Old Woman I Know is your guide through the first three important people of the Super Seven! And I have one significant piece of information for you. Study it carefully and patiently before you give your first answer," he said, as he handed her a scroll and took Obadiah in exchange, placing him over his shoulder. "We'll return for you after your test. Tally Ho!!, my Mighty Mustard Seed!

And remember: It's not what you know now that counts; it's what you're going to know!"

"Make sure my dog is here when I get back!" Bethany said. After a moment of further thought, Bethany continued, "Wait, where do I want to be, and what happens if I don't figure it out?" she said, as Gabriel began to adjust the JOY device and with a "zap" disappeared. Bethany was left alone with only Gabriel's "signature" blue butterflies swirling around her head. She watched them disappear one by one as she wondered whether she would be up to the challenge. After almost a minute of total silence, Bethany began to hear a noise like footsteps behind her. Turning around, she spotted a very old woman slowly approaching her. Her hair was gray and her sea green eyes shone intensely, penetrating Bethany's every bone. She was dressed in traditional Hebrew dress with a cloth draped around her body. She pointed to Bethany and then to a door in the Temple as she spoke the word "Larcel!"

Bethany did not know what to make of this woman and her word. She then decided that a bit of formal introduction was in order. "Hi! I'm Bethany. You must be Old Woman I Know. I mean, I don't know you, and you really don't look that old, but I believe that Gabriel said that was your name. You do know Gabriel, don't you?"

"Ingtrain!" the old woman said emphatically, as she opened a door and pointed to stairs that appeared to lead to a passageway below the Temple.

"Excuse me, I don't understand what you mean."

"Ingtrain! Ingtrain! Now!" The old lady said raising her voice to almost a shrill echoing off the Temple walls. She again motioned towards the stairs.

"OK, OK, I can take a hint. I'm leaving, although I don't know where I'm going or why." Bethany thought to herself, "If this person is supposed to help me learn anything and get me through this mess, I'm in serious trouble. Her vocabulary is strange, although I must say she gives strong visual signals."

Following the old lady through the underground maze below was difficult. It was extremely dark and the maze wound around with paths leading in different directions every twenty yards or so. Suddenly, the old lady turned to Bethany and said, "Stop here! Ingtrain, now. "Suddenly, Bethany realized that in front of her were three iron gates with bars, which rose to the height of the cave. She could barely see in the distance the last gate. Again the old lady said "Ingtrain, now!" The old lady then held up a single index finger in the air and said "First sonper! Braaham! Peatre this!"

Bethany felt herself becoming more and more frustrated as she was bombarded with the nonsensical words that the old lady threw her way. "I must think," she reflected. "Old Woman I Know must be speaking in tongues or something," she thought to herself. She wondered what Gabriel would do in this situation. As Bethany looked up from her deep reflection, she saw the old lady looking straight at her with her hands folded, showing what Bethany thought must be the universal sign of prayer. Hesitating for a moment, Bethany finally asked the old lady "Should I pray?" The lady nodded in the affirmative. Bethany began her prayer, and, somewhat to her surprise, her mind drifted for a moment to her family. She thanked God for her wonderful parents and for her brother and sister, then realizing how much they meant to her. She went on to thank the Lord for each day of her life. She also asked for wisdom and patience in addressing the challenge at hand.

After several minutes of prayer, she opened her eyes, refreshed as she once again focused on the task before her. For the first time, the old lady was smiling at her and gave her a "thumbs up," which Bethany interpreted to mean that she was on the right track. Bethany then recalled that she had yet to open the scroll that Gabriel had left her. Unrolling the scroll, she read it out loud as it echoed off the cave walls:

Two Kings, each with arms extended,

New King holds Father Abe and me,
Sling King holds Father Abe and He;

Know when you are?
Then time to know when Father Abe he be;

Know when New King be?
Then know that Sling King stands balanced 'tween
Abe and He;

Open wide His arms for all to see,
New King's arms extended to infinity;

Close His hands in prayerful reflection;
And you'll see Abe as a powerful connection.

Identify the Kings and Abe he be,
And receive the keys to open gates – all three!

"Oh, Gabriel, why did you do this to me? An old lady teacher who speaks in tongues and my lifeline is a riddle!" Bethany began studying the words closely – contemplating any possibility.

Then Old Woman I Know said once again, holding her index finger high in the air. "First, Braaham, You are in ingtrain!" Bethany recalled that the old woman, according to Gabriel had some type of speech problem and then noticed something very interesting – possibly a pattern of speech. She understood each of the one-syllable words that the old lady said, but the multiple syllable words seemed garbled. Gabriel said the old woman was honest so she would answer truthfully any question asked. Bethany thought about what questions she should ask to test her theory.

"Ms. Old Woman I Know, ma'am, could you please tell me if you know Gabriel?" she said, trying to be as respectful as possible.

"Yes, I know him well." (Bethany thought that her theory had merit – all one-syllable words made sense so far. She must push her to speak a two-syllable word to test her theory further.)

Ma'am, could you please tell me if Gabriel, in your opinion, is honest or dishonest?"

"Well, I would say he is as esthon as they come. He is just derwonful!"

Bethany let these words sink in, as she processed the information she had received and her mind began to put the pieces of the puzzle together. Suddenly, as she realized the answer, Bethany leaped for joy. "It worked, it worked!" she yelled, as she danced around the cave and then broke into something between a chant and a song. " I figgg-ured-it-out, I figgg-ured-it-out, yes I did, I did, I did! Oh, I'm just so won-der-ful, so, so won-der-ful to meeee, yes I am! I'm so, so won-der-ful to meeee – yeah, yeah, yeah ... Yeah!!!"

As Bethany pranced about, the old woman watched with a slight grin on her face but tried not to show it. Calming down for a moment, Bethany realized that she had only won half the battle and began to address again the riddle and her oral clues. Focusing on the word "Braaham," she began to transpose various combinations of letters and syllables in her mind and then saw the word she was searching for. Finally, turning to Old Woman I Know, she said, "I think the 'me' part of the riddle is me and the 'Abe' part is father Abraham. And you said "First, Braaham," and that must mean that Abraham is the first person of my Super Seven list! Am I right?"

Old Woman I Know smiled and said, "Yes, you are right, my Orfaved One. Urefig out the two Kings and get the keys for the three gates, but do not getfor the dates!"

"Oh, yeah, don't forget the dates. Right! Got it. This is derwonful!" Bethany said getting into the groove. Then she once again focused on the riddle. She pulled out a piece of paper that she found in her Bible and a pen that Gabriel had previously given her. Next she drew two stick men to help her better understand the riddle. Although the cave was dark with only small lamps about, her eyes had adjusted to the dim light. Her men looked like this:

Bethany continued to think it through step by step, mumbling to herself. "Well, I know now that Abe is Father Abraham. The riddle says 'know when you are, then time to

know when Abe he be.' So if 'you' in the riddle is me, then father Abraham must be about 2000 B.C., the opposite of when I live kind of, since I'm in about 2000 A.D."

Bethany thought hard as she closed her eyes and attempted to visualize a king, with outstretched arms, holding Abraham in one hand and her in the other. Then she saw the beautiful connection, commenting out loud "That would make the New King – Jesus – since he was born just in the middle. And if Jesus closes his hands in prayer then Father Abraham and I are brought together. I get it. That's cool!"

"Do not getfor Sling King," the old woman reminded Bethany, smiling at her slightly.

"Oh, yeah, who is the Sling King?" Bethany then walked about studying the drawing she had made and the riddle on the scroll as she continued to talk to herself. "The Sling King stands balanced between Abe and 'He' who has to be the New King – Jesus. And this Sling King must be around 1000 B.C. since he is right between Abe and Jesus. But who is he?" Then she remembered something that Gabriel had taught her looking at Jacob's (Israel's) family tree. Jesus traced his ancestry back to the tribe of Judah and King David. And since she remembered how close he was to God, she thought David might be the Sling King, especially since he had killed Goliath with a rock using a slingshot device. So she decided to go with David.

"Time ningrun out!" the gray haired lady said with a high-pitched voice.

Bethany cleared her throat as she spoke, "Ms. Old Woman I Know, I think the answers are all on this little chart," which she completed as she talked and then gave it to her.

2000 B.C.		2000 A.D.
Abraham	Jesus	Bethany

o———————————0———————————o

```
            1000 B.C.
Abraham      David       Jesus
o—————————0—————————o
```

"Am I right?" Bethany inquired with some confidence.

The old woman said, "You are rectcor!"

Bethany hesitated as she tried to make certain she understood the response and then suddenly squealed with delight, "I am rectcor! I got it! I got it! I am correct!"

The old woman went on, "You have the keys that peno the three gates. God bless you my child, and good luck with your testcon!" She next handed Bethany the keys and gave her a big hug. Then with a smile, she waved as she turned and walked away.

As Bethany took the first key and inserted it into the first gate, the words "Gate of Abraham" mystically appeared at the top, and the large gate swung open. As she walked to the other side, out of the corner of her eye she spotted three large lions, four bears and a pack of seven wolves coming out of the darkness and beginning to block her path to the next gate. She became frightened as she wondered whether she should retreat to behind the Gate of Abraham for safety. Closing her eyes, she prayed for a sign as to what to do. Opening her eyes, she collected her courage and decided to take one more step towards the beasts hoping they would (for some reason – any reason) back away from the next gate. To her dismay, the wolves began to growl and hunched low as they circled her. As the lions held their ground in front of the next gate, the four bears brought their bodies to full height by standing on their hind legs as if in defiance of her advance.

Bethany began to question what she should do next. Suddenly, out of nowhere came a large old man and, as he approached her, he asked her for his keys. Without a word, she gave them to him, since a small voice inside her told her to do so. For some reason she then asked him, "Sir, could you help me get through those gates because, well, it's important. You see, I'm training for a contest."

"I've heard all about it. Follow me," he said, as he motioned for her to follow him through a passageway that led to the next gate. "Do not for any reason look back!" he said sternly, as they moved forward. Miraculously, the animals backed away as he led Bethany forward to the second gate. Upon his insertion of the key, the top of the second gate burst into flames and the fire seared the words "Gate of Moses" at the top. The old man calmly signaled for her to pass through.

Moving forward toward the third gate, the snarling animals followed them closely – so closely that Bethany could feel the hot air from their breaths on the back side of her body. As instructed, she did not look back and felt a strange calm come over her as they approached the third gate. Viewing it, she wondered whose name would appear as the gate was opened. She didn't have to wait long. As soon as the old man inserted the key, the words "Gate of Joshua" appeared at the top. Immediately, the gate began to quiver and shake violently and then it suddenly crumbled into a thousand pieces. Escorting her past the remaining rubble of the gate, the old man then turned and said to her with a slight smile, "Not bad work, kid – especially for a rookie. You made the cut. But don't forget what you've learned. We all need a little help and guidance sometimes. It's all around you, if you just take time to look and ask. Well, got my keys and got to go now. Good luck, Favored One! Oh, I forgot – take the stairs to leave and shut the door on your way out."

Almost in a daze, she complied and went up the stairs briskly, finding the door and opening it quickly. Passing through the door, she realized that she was back in the Temple on the other side of the room that she had left! Gabriel was waiting for her there.

Running to greet him, she said, "Gabriel I made it! I made it!"

Gabriel gave her a huge bear hug, and said, "I'm so proud of you. I can tell you, we're poppin'!! Big Time! Way to go there partner. We're going to be ready for this contest. We sure are!" Forgetting themselves, they began to prance around the room inside the Temple. Obadiah tried to join in the celebration by jumping up on their legs as they danced around. And then he did his infamous "walk like Gabriel" routine and fell over flat on his side. Gabriel and Bethany broke into laughter at his frolics.

Finally they calmed down and Bethany had to ask, "Gabriel, the old man with the keys, who was he? I mean, he said the keys were his. So I gave them to him."

"I didn't know anything about any man being with Old Woman I Know. She was supposed to be alone. Maybe someone borrowed his keys, and he wanted them back. Jumpin' Jehoshaphat! I just don't know. Who was that masked man, Tonto?"

"Quit fooling around, Gabriel, and quit that funny talk. I want to know!"

"Sorry, I guess you do. But I really don't know. There are some mysteries in life to which even angels don't have the answer. Maybe in time it will be revealed to you. Anyway, I'm awfully proud of you for completing your mission. Hey, let's have a snack to celebrate! I've got a couple of food party favors that you'll just love," he said, pulling a few seeds from his back pocket and studying them carefully for his menu selection.

Chapter 14
The Super Seven

After some food and a short break, Gabriel stretched his arms wide. Viewing the sky from the Temple, Gabriel saw a single cloud in the distance on this hot afternoon. "Time to get back to your training and the Super Seven list," he said to Bethany. Pulling out a chart from his back pocket, Gabriel unfolded it for her to see. The dates prior to 1000 B.C. are real hard to pin down because of the scarcity of evidence of early events. But the dates I've chosen, which are rounded to the nearest century, should be acceptable for purposes of your contest. And note on Abraham that I could have picked any date from 2100 B.C. to 1700 B.C. for when he probably lived. That's what your Bible scholars have come up with, although they really don't know for sure. Of course, I like the year 2000 B.C. for him, since it has such beautiful symmetry with your time."

"Oh, yes. Old Woman I Know taught me that, along with your little riddle. Abe and I are the same distance apart from Jesus. I really can't forget that. And David is in the middle of Abe and Jesus, like 1000 B.C. That's pretty easy to remember."

"Good, lock that in, Bethany, while we look at this chart. Remember, this is the Old Testament so focus on David, the Sling King, with his arms wide open here."

THE FAMILY'S
SUPER SEVEN LIST

	LAW	
2000 B.C. and earlier	Genesis	1. 2000 B.C. Abraham/HEBREWS FIRST LIVE IN CANAAN
	Exodus	
1400-1300 B.C.	Leviticus	2. 1400 B.C. Moses/DEPARTURE FROM EGYPT
	Numbers	
	Deuteronomy	
	HISTORY	
	Joshua	
1300-1000 B.C.	Judges	3. 1300 B.C. Joshua/REENTER CANAAN: JERICHO
	Ruth	
1000 B.C.	I Samuel	4. 1000 B.C. David/UNITED KINGDOM
	II Samuel	-Saul before David; -Solomon after
1000-500 B.C.	I Kings	5. 700 B.C. Isaiah/FALL of ISRAEL -Defeated by the Assyrians
	II Kings	
	I Chronicles	6. 600 B.C. Jeremiah/FALL of JUDAH -Defeated by the Babylonians
	II Chronicles	
500-400 B.C.	Ezra	7. 500 B.C. Nehemiah/RETURN AND REBUILD TEMPLE WALLS
	Nehemiah	- Persia King Cyrus permitted Jews' return
	Esther	

Bethany viewed the list of dates next to the books of the Law and History. "Hey, wait a minute, you left out the five books of Poetry – Job, Psalms, Proverbs, Ecclesiastes and Song of Solomon. When were they written?"

"I'll let you figure that out. Here's a clue. You know that David wrote many of the Psalms and often sang them to Saul while playing his harp. And tradition has it that King Solomon, David's son, wrote parts of Proverbs, Ecclesiastes and the Song of Solomon."

"Yes, I remember learning about David singing Psalms in Sunday school. I guess it would make sense that Solomon might have written some of Proverbs since those are wise sayings. And, of course, the Song of Solomon is logically Solomon's song. Right?"

"Right!" Gabriel said encouragingly. "Now, while some parts were written later, you know when many parts of the early Psalms, Proverbs, Ecclesiastes and the Song of Solomon were written, since you know roughly when Saul, David and Solomon lived – that is, the only three kings of the united kingdom."

Bethany paused, "1000 B.C.?" Bethany answered timidly.

"Of course!" Gabriel responded. "Why were you so hesitant?"

"That seemed easy since I remembered when David lived. I thought it might be a trick question."

"Oh, good, good. You should watch out for those. Sometimes a question that looks easy is actually much more difficult than it first appears. For example, I said when were the 'early' Psalms written. Many of the Psalms were written much later than 1000 B.C., so it's important to listen carefully to the question asked. Take your time. Remember the tortoise and the bear!" Gabriel said. "Now, study these dates, people and events closely, and I will ask you one more question to make sure you understand how to use this information as the branches of your Christmas tree."

"Speaking of Christmas," Bethany said, "I have a question."

Gabriel closed his eyes tightly and cringed a little as he prepared himself for the "Is there really a Santa Claus" inquiry. After a long pause, Gabriel asked, "What's that?"

"Well, if the New Testament begins with the life of Jesus, which is about 400 years later, why does the Old Testament History stop around 400 B.C.?"

"What a good question!" Gabriel responded, delighted to be back on track. "Unfortunately, I don't have a good answer for you. Possibly this period was not considered significant enough to be included in the Bible; you know, maybe there weren't any great Prophets during that period. Although I must say that several books on the Apocrypha – the books that didn't make the major leagues ... err, the canon – have some interesting stories during this period, especially the period of the Maccabees revolt."

"OK," she answered slowly, reflecting on what he had just said. "There's that word 'canon' again. It kind of throws me for a loop."

"I understand how it might. Just remember those are the major league books of the Bible – at least for you Protestants."

After a pause, Bethany said, "Hey wait, coach. This contest I've entered – is it going to be like Bible Jeopardy? I mean, will the judges give me the answer, and I give them the question?"

"Well, not exactly," Gabriel said, looking down and rubbing his hand across the cool, gold-covered floor of the Temple.

"It's not? Well, what's it like then? Is it like what I had to do with Old Woman I Know?" Bethany inquired, a little nervous because of this new development.

Gabriel reflected, as he looked around the room. "It's more like ... like ... 'Twenty Questions,' I guess."

"Twenty Questions?" Bethany inquired anxiously. "Oral or written?"

"Oral, I think."

"Oral? Well, can I just 'pass' if I don't know the answer? I mean, is this going to be like a cross-examination or what? Will there be one word answers or discussions? How about multiple choice? I like multiple choice," she rambled on, half-afraid to stop to hear what Gabriel would say next.

"I really don't know, Bethany."

"Don't know! Don't know! How come you don't know? I mean, you're my coach aren't you? You're supposed to know these things!" Bethany's voice raised to almost a shout.

"Bethany, calm down! Calm down! You're upsetting yourself unnecessarily. It's just a little contest. I mean it's not going to decide whether you get into heaven or not. It's not even going to make a difference as to which college will accept you. Dear child, take hold of yourself! Do your best. That's all I ask."

Bethany began to settle down, as she once again viewed the beautiful interior of the Temple. "I guess you're right. I mean it's not a question that's likely to be on my college application." She breathed deeply twice and then said, "I don't know, I guess I get a little too excited over things. Like I can't even take the 'SAT' – you know, the test you have to take to get into college – until at least a year from now, and I'm already worried. Do you think that I'm hyper? I mean, my parents say that I should relax more. But I'm thinking about an Ivy League school or a top-notch state university. I figure if I study hard, make all A's and start preparing for my college boards when I hit the seventh grade – well, maybe I've got a shot at those schools. Oh, of course, I'm working on my basketball every day – always the possibility of a scholarship. And you know, a kid needs some scholarship or aid money to help the folks with their financial burdens. I mean, unless parents start saving by the time their oldest gets to first grade, college is going to be a real hardship. My folks only started this year, and they're in real trouble the way I see it."

Gabriel could take no more. He gently covered her mouth with his left hand and raised the forefinger of his right straight up in front of his protruding lips, as he said "Shhh, let's live a little more one day at a time. Planning for the future is a good idea, but why don't you wait until you're a parent to worry about such things?"

"That's what my folks always say, but I can see they're going to need some help. What do you think?"

"I think you should listen to your parents," Gabriel said without hesitation. "Do the best you can and don't worry about it. Remember, however, education is a constant exercise – not just something you do in school. Where you live, with the resources generally available, everyone can and should keep studying, expanding his or her knowledge. And not just so that you can get a better job and make more money, but for the sheer joy of knowing, understanding how things work, why things are as they are . . ." Gabriel reflected and then smiling said, "Bethany, you've done it again! How did I become your guidance counselor?"

"I'm not certain. But since you are, do you have any tips on the best college buys for the new millennium?" she laughed, jokingly.

"Enough! Enough" Gabriel went on, "Let's get back to basics. OK, now it's important that your training include physical as well as mental activities. God often selects people of action, so I'm thinking that the contest might require some physical as well as intellectual activity. There are number of tasks that you may be asked to perform, and you must be ready for any challenge. Two instruments that you will train with are in that container over there," he said pointing to a small black box laying only a few feet away. "Go open it and bring me its contents."

Bethany complied and opened the box. "Gabriel, these are beautiful," she said as she held the two instruments in her hand.

"Yes, wonderful replicas of Moses' rod and David's sling. I'm giving them to you now as a kind of graduation gift for passing your first test. Nice aren't they? I had them made especially for you, based on your size and weight. And the rod has an extra special feature: It can be folded into a small umbrella size. Now you must learn to handle these correctly for the contest. Both the rod and the sling should be used only as instruments of protection and leadership." Never, never use them in anger. You must learn to control them. They must not control you. Understand?"

"Wow! This is poppin'!!" Bethany exclaimed, as she examined her new accessories closely.

"Ah! Another new expression. What does it mean? And what is its origin?"

"Well ... my friends and I kind of made it up. It means really exciting, like when you put popcorn in the microwave, and its popping so hard the bag is jumping around inside, and you can't wait for it to stop."

"Oh ... poppin'! I get it! That's a good one all right!"

"Coach," Bethany said reflecting on her physical training and the contest, "what's this special training all about? I mean this isn't like the gladiators versus the Christians, is it?"

"Oh, no. That's New Testament stuff. If things get physical, it will be more like David and Goliath or the tribes versus the Philistines. We've got to be ready for anything! This is the first contest you know, and we haven't many details."

"I'll be ready. I like to work hard. I train for basketball every day. I'm in pretty good shape, if I do say so myself," she concluded as she took the rod and pointed it toward

Oba as he put his shoulders and head down and began to bark and jump around playfully at Bethany. "Oh, this is sweet," she continued as she waved the rod in the air and whipped it around her head a few times like a samurai warrior trained in the martial arts. "May the force be with you, Gabriel."

"Huh?"

"You know – 'Star Wars.'"

"Star Wars? What were the Star Wars?"

"Gabriel, you've got to get out more often! You don't know about Star Wars? That was huge! I mean it's like you've been in a time warp or something."

"Well, yes. I guess, in a matter of speaking, I have. I've really got some holes in my knowledge of recent earth history, although I've been trying to catch up. I can't believe that I missed a series of wars on your planet," shaking his head with some confusion.

"They weren't real wars. It was just a movie about the future, and they had these cool lasers and … and … they … they … oh, well, never mind. It's not really that important," Bethany commented, realizing that she had a lot to do to prepare for the contest. "What exercises do I have to do to get myself in peak condition?"

Gabriel thought for a moment. Tapping his finger to his lips a few times before he spoke, he finally said, " I will take you to a training area near here. Once there, while doing your memory work, you must pick up progressively heavier stones and move them to a place that I will designate. After you move each stone, you must take your rod and strike both sides of the rock," Gabriel said. To demonstrate, he located a decorative urn in the corner of the Temple, and pretended to strike both sides of the vase which acted as his imaginary rock. "Careful," he continued, "not too hard and not too soft. Just right. See. You must learn control." After several more demonstrations, Bethany, although thinking it rather odd, tried the exercise over and over while she stood in the Temple. At the same time she listened to Gabriel spout off Bible history, as he attempted to train her mind and her body.

"Oh, I get it. Cross training! Right?" Bethany said, finally understanding the concept, although still thinking it strange indeed.

"Well ... yes, cross training!"

"When do I get to do a full workout with my rod and sling?"

"Now's as good a time as any. I tell you what, stand by my side, and I'll transport us to a great training location just about fifteen miles from here." Bethany obliged and clapping her hands for her dog to come, Oba leaped into her arms. After a moment, they were zapped to their new destination near Jerusalem.

Chapter 15
Squished, Squashed, Squeezed

Their new location was at an oasis just outside the town of Jericho. The area was stunning, with palm trees and green vegetation everywhere – in stark contrast to the outlying desert that could be seen in the distance.

Bethany thought this place must be a bit like spring training camp for professional baseball players in Florida and was ready to comment on her observation when Gabriel interjected, "Now, let's get on with it. No time to waste." Pointing to a pile of stones nearby, Gabriel added, "Start moving those rocks to that area over there, and I'll have you practice with your rod and sling while you study your lesson. With practice you should be able to take a pebble, place it in your sling and strike an object – like that tree over there – from a distance of forty-five feet." Gabriel again focused on the 'Super Seven' list before speaking further.

THE FAMILY'S
<u>SUPER SEVEN LIST</u>

	<u>LAW</u>	
2000 B.C. and earlier	Genesis	1. 2000 B.C. <u>Abraham</u>/HEBREWS FIRST LIVE IN CANAAN
1400-1300 B.C.	Exodus Leviticus Numbers Deuteronomy	2. 1400 B.C. <u>Moses</u>/DEPARTURE FROM EGYPT

	<u>HISTORY</u>	
1300-1000 B.C.	Joshua Judges Ruth	3. 1300 B.C. <u>Joshua</u>/REENTER CANAAN: JERICHO
1000 B.C.	I Samuel II Samuel	4. 1000 B.C. <u>David</u>/UNITED KINGDOM -Saul before David; -Solomon after
1000-500 B.C.	I Kings II Kings	5. 700 B.C. <u>Isaiah</u>/FALL of ISRAEL -Defeated by the Assyrians
	I Chronicles II Chronicles	6. 600 B.C. <u>Jeremiah</u>/FALL of JUDAH -Defeated by the Babylonians
500-400 B.C.	Ezra Nehemiah Esther	7. 500 B.C.<u>Nehemiah</u>/RETURN AND REBUILD TEMPLE WALLS - Persia King Cyrus permitted Jews' return

2000 B.C. and earlier	Genesis	1. 2000 B.C. <u>Abraham</u>/HEBREWS FIRST LIVE IN CANAAN
1400-1300 B.C.	Exodus Leviticus Numbers	2. 1400 B.C. <u>Moses</u>/DEPARTURE FROM EGYPT

"OK. Now using the dates, people and events I have given you to memorize, logically what was the time period in which Samuel lived, roughly speaking?"

"Gabriel, this is too hard. I can't figure this out. There's too much information on this chart!"

"Oh, I see your point. Well, just focus on the seven dates and people next to those dates first. Ignore everything else. OK? Maybe you might like this version," he said as he drew a much simpler time line on the bottom of the chart.

Abraham	Moses		David		Jeremiah	
2000 B.C	1400		1000		600	

o————————o————o———o———o————·o———o

		Joshua		Isaiah	Nehemiah
		1300		700	500

"Now try again and think, child ... think!"

Bethany again viewed the chart and this time studied it more carefully. After a few moments, she said, "Well, since the date for David is 1000 B.C., I would think Samuel would be just a few years earlier since he was the Prophet that appointed Saul as Israel's first king, and Saul and David were living at the same time."

"Not only that, Samuel was actually living when David was a young lad," Gabriel added. "Remember, once Saul fell out of favor with God, Samuel went to David while he was still a shepherd and anointed him with oil. This meant that God had selected David to succeed Saul."

"And before Saul were the judges who are discussed in the book of Judges. Right, Coach?" Bethany said, pleased with her response.

"Oh, you are getting good at this game!" Gabriel responded. "While the tribes of Israel didn't have a king before Saul, they did have leaders from various tribes who were rather informally recognized as the main spokesperson for the tribes on important military and administrative-legal functions. There were quite a few of these so-called judges after Joshua, but he was so important that he got a book of the Bible named for him. By the way, did you know that Jesus' name in Hebrew is 'Joshua?'"

"No, I didn't. But I did know that Joshua was the one who led the tribes of Israel into the Promised Land and fought the Canaanites and won the battle of Jericho and ..."

"And the walls came tumbling down!" Gabriel said finishing Bethany's statement. "Precisely! Then Gabriel added, "Joshua, as you will recall, was from the tribe of Ephraim."

"Wasn't Ephraim one of the sons of Joseph, along with Manasseh?" she interjected.

"Yes, that's right," Gabriel confirmed as he nodded.

"Gee, I bet Joseph would have been proud of his grandson, Joshua. I mean his great, great ... How many greats would that be anyway?"

"Let's just say his multiple great grandson and leave it at that. But, anyway, there were other tribes that had their heroes too. Many of these people were "judges" and were leaders for the tribes. Three you should definitely know are Deborah, Gideon, and, last but certainly not least, Samson."

"Oh, everybody knows about Samson. Which tribe was he from?"

Now Bethany, I'll let you take an educated guess," Gabriel said as he withdrew from his back pocket the map of the twelve tribes he had shown her previously.

Bethany reviewed the map. As she began to use her binary and then macro association, she thought, "Samson and Delilah – who was Delilah? Was she from a tribe of Israel? No, that didn't make sense; she was helping Samson's enemy, the Philistines. So she was probably a Philistine too. But how does that tell me which tribe Samson would be from?" She reviewed the map once again, closely locating the land of the Philistines. After a few more

moments of thought, a smile burst out on her face. "I've narrowed it down to one of three tribes: Dan, Judah or Simeon. Right?"

"Very good. How did you know that?"

"Well, I remembered that Samson fought the Philistines, and I figured that the tribes closest to the Philistines' property would be the most logical choice."

"Now, do you want to take a guess as to which of those three tribes is the right answer?" Gabriel said encouragingly.

Bethany paused and then said, "Dan?"

"Bravo!" Gabriel yelled, "How in the name of Samson did you figure that one out?"

"Well, the Philistines had beachfront property so I'm sure everyone wanted it. You know, the condomania problem." Gabriel looked interested as she continued. "But it looked like to me that Dan's tribe had the smallest piece of land and was probably kinda squenched up and needed all the property they could get. Plus, you told me earlier that the tribe of Dan and the Philistines had fought before. Remember?"

"Not bad!" said Gabriel. "But what do the words 'squenched up' mean?"

"It means really squished tight. You know, squashed."

"I thought squash was a vegetable," Gabriel responded curiously.

"It is, but it also means squeezed or flattened, I think."

"Oh, I see, compressed and contained in a small area," Gabriel concluded, as he wrapped his arms around himself and squeezed tightly. "Squenched, that's a new one on me. What's the past perfect of squench?"

"Huh?" Bethany responded.

"Oh, never mind. Let's get on with our lesson. Let's talk about Gideon who was from the tribe of Manasseh. He was special and, although his faith was weak for a while, he became devoted to God and totally confident in the Lord's word. With only 300 of his bravest and most devoted men, Gideon drove out the invading foreigners from across the Jordan River, even though they outnumbered his men by the thousands. Let's read about him in Judges. Chapter 6 might be a good place to start," he said handing her his Bible.

As requested, Bethany read several wonderful stories about Gideon. Her favorite was when he met an angel of the Lord face-to-face – just like Bethany had done. Completing this assignment, she read other parts of the book of Judges and then had a question for Gabriel. "Hey, Coach! You mentioned that Deborah was a judge. Was Deborah a woman? I mean, was she really important 'cause it seems that I haven't heard many Bible stories about important women. In fact, my mom says that if there had been an EEOC back then, the history of the world would have been a lot different."

"What's the EEOC?"

"Oh, it's this federal government commission that tries to make sure everybody's equal ... especially women."

"Equal to what?"

"Equal to men, of course!" Bethany responded incredulously. "Don't you know about these things?"

"No. No, I don't. Tell me about it," Gabriel asked, curious as usual.

"Well, this commission is supposed to make sure that 'everybody's equal on compensation' ... that's what EEOC stands for, I think. You see, if a woman does the same job a man does, she should get the same pay. Women are supposed to have the same rights and opportunities as men in America."

"That sounds reasonable," Gabriel interjected.

"But my uncle thinks it's a bad idea."

"He does?"

"Well, yes. He says if women are paid the same thing for jobs as men, they will all want to go to work full time, and then who will take care of the kids? He says this society is almost at the 'rent a parent' stage already. He told me this story about this boy who was in high school causing big problems for his teachers. So the teachers call up the parents for a meeting at the school to discuss the situation. The meeting date is set and, on the day of the meeting, guess who shows up?"

"I don't know. Who?"

"The parents' lawyer! Can you believe that?"

"No! That's terrible! Why didn't the parents attend?"

"I don't know. Uncle Lot bets it's because the father was too busy negotiating a big company deal and the mother was called out of town on an emergency meeting for her job."

"Oh. Is this the global parent situation we discussed previously?"

"Well, kind of. But my mom says the blame can't be laid on working women that easily. She says it's a two-way street and my uncle and men like him continue to drive right down the middle, ignoring the white line."

After a long pause, Gabriel decided that it was best to get back to his subject. "Listen, Bethany, I don't know what, if anything, Deborah got paid, but she was important. You see, she was from the tribe of Ephraim and had its powerful army at her disposal, along with the armies of Manasseh and Benjamin."

"Why was that?" she inquired.

"You mean, why did the tribes of Manasseh and Benjamin follow Ephraim?" Bethany nodded. "Well," Gabriel continued, "it goes back to family relationships really. At least, this is my best guess. The Manasseh relationship is easy. Manasseh and Ephraim were full-blooded brothers, the two sons of Joseph, remember?" he said as he pulled out the family tree map, and then continued.

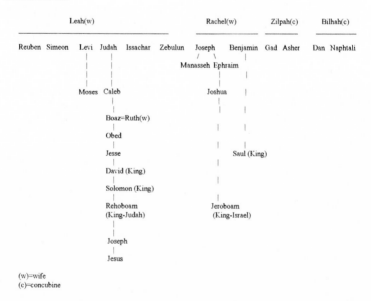

(w)=wife
(c)=concubine

"The Benjamin connection takes a little more explanation," he said. "Joseph had only one true full-blooded brother and that was his younger brother,

Benjamin. That is, both were the sons of Jacob and Jacob's second wife, Rachel," Gabriel said pointing to the family tree under Rachel. So it was natural that Joseph's sons and Benjamin would likely stick together."

"Oh, yeah, now I can see why," Bethany commented with some confidence.

"Anyway, the very northern tribes of Naphtali and Zebulun were being threatened by the army of the Canaanites led by a general named Sisera. But the general for Naphtali, named Barak, was afraid to start any war with Sisera since Sisera was, how do you say it? – one mean hombre, and had instructed his men to take no prisoners! Anyone captured was immediately tortured and killed!"

"Hey, wait a minute, that's against the Geneva Convention and a major war crime! Didn't Sisera know that?"

"Remember, we're talking 1300 to 1200 B.C. here. Not only wasn't there a Geneva Convention yet, there wasn't even a Geneva, Switzerland, I dare say." Gabriel paused to let this point sink in before he continued. "Well, Barak just flat told Deborah 'I won't go unless you go with me!' Of course, Deborah said she'd go, and with God on their side, they defeated Sisera."

"No kidding! You mean this big general wouldn't go to war unless Deborah went with him? That's totally rad! My Uncle Lot's not going to believe this one! Are you sure?"

"Read it for yourself. It's Judges, Chapter 4," he said, as he again gave her his small Bible and lightly placed it into her lap next to Oba. "Before you look that up, I think I'll transport us back to the Temple in Jerusalem. I sensed something unusual was going on there when we left, and I'd like to check it out. Ready for your next *JOY* ride?"

"Let's really *enJOY it!*" Bethany said with enthusiasm as she grabbed Obadiah, and they disappeared with a blinding light.

Chapter 16
If You Go With Me, I Will Go

Walking toward the front of the Temple, Gabriel viewed the scene in the courtyard from his vantage point inside. The activity had definitely picked up outside. People were scurrying around looking concerned and confused. Merchants suddenly were starting to pack their goods and looked as if they were preparing to leave. "Something's going on out there, but I'm not sure what," Gabriel said softly as he turned, scratched his head and walked back toward Bethany only to find her engrossed in her reading. She was still reading Judges and finally came to Chapter 4, verse 8:

> Barak said to her, "If you will go with me, I will go; but if you will not go with me, I will not go."

Bethany smiled as she shook her head with great satisfaction. "That's what it says all right! That Deborah is something else! She's awesome!"

"And she's not the only heroine in the Old Testament,"

Gabriel interjected. "There's Ruth and Esther, to name a few more. Ruth is important in a different kind of way."

"How's that?"

"Well, for one thing, if it weren't for her, you might say that this Temple may never have been built."

"I don't understand. David designed and built the Temple didn't he? What's Ruth got to do with anything?"

"Correction, Bethany," Gabriel said. "David designed the Temple, and Solomon had it built. But anyway, what if David had never been born?"

"Oh, I see." Bethany said, reflecting on his statement. "So Ruth was his mother or grandmother or something."

"Close." Gabriel said coaxingly, "Go back further."

"Great grandmother?"

"You got it! Bravo!"

"And that's why the book of Ruth is before Samuel. It's logical, right?" Bethany said, asking for confirmation. "Since Samuel lived during the time of David."

"Bethany, you're running on all cylinders!"

Bethany and Gabriel sat quietly for a moment smiling at each other. Both began to realize how close they were becoming as they shared their experiences and knowledge. After a few moments of silence, Gabriel spoke up, "Bethany, you're quite a trooper."

"Thanks, Coach. You know, maybe I could win that contest. Wouldn't it be great if I could slam dunk one of those college professor types!"

"Bethany, I can tell you're someone that can ..." he searched for an American phrase to drive home the point, "bring home the bacon!"

Sometimes Bethany couldn't quite understand Gabriel. Why would she want to do that? She didn't especially like bacon and, besides, it wasn't very good for you – too greasy and too much fat.

"Oh, Bethany. I forgot to tell you another reason why Ruth was so important. Remember 'AMEM.' I used it as a memory aid for the non-Israelite people who lived in the region on the east side of the Jordan River."

"Well, yes. I remember – all those 'ites' people. But what's that got to do with Ruth?"

"Remember what the first 'M' in AMEM stands for?"

Bethany thought, and then said cautiously, "The Moabites?"

"That's right. The Moabites. Now guess who was a Moabite."

"Not Ruth?" Bethany said astonished.

"Yes, Ruth."

"You mean … you mean that David wasn't a full-blooded Jew? I mean he wasn't even a full-blooded Hebrew then was he?"

"Well, that's right, if you define a Hebrew as a direct descendant of Abraham. As you will recall, the Moabites were descendants of Lot, Abraham's nephew, who ended up settling on the southeast side of the Jordan River. Lot wasn't very religious and don't forget that it was Abraham's descendants that were promised the land."

"Gee. That must have been embarrassing for the Jews to find out that David's great grandmother was a Moabite. Did they try to cover it up?"

"Nope. They even put it in the Bible. In the last chapter of Ruth, I believe."

"What! Why did they do that? I don't understand these people. They leave out hundreds of years of perfectly good history and decide to stick in something like that. It just doesn't figure!" Bethany said as she shook her head, looking perplexed, and then lowered her brows as she pinched her lower lip tightly.

"Au contraire! It does figure, and I'll tell you why," Gabriel responded. "The book of Ruth goes into great detail. You see, Ruth was as good, as loyal, as kind a person as any you could find. She married a Jewish man whose parents had left their land due to a famine and had come to her family's land, the land of the Moabites, where there was food. Unfortunately, her husband died leaving her and her widowed mother-in-law, Naomi, in Moab. When Naomi told Ruth that she was returning to Judah, Ruth insisted on going with her to take care of her, even though Naomi had no sons living in Judah or elsewhere for Ruth to marry. Ruth didn't care. She said that Naomi's people would be her people and the God of Israel would be her God. So Ruth left Moab and went to Judah where she ended up marrying a relative of Naomi. It's really a delightful story with a happy ending."

"I bet she ended up marrying Prince Charming or something like that, didn't she?"

"Well, almost. You see, Ruth ends up marrying Boaz, a rich relative of Naomi's deceased husband, who was a kind and generous man. And out of Ruth's second marriage she has a son, Obed, who has a son, Jesse, who has a son, the great King David! And Ruth was important because her story showed that the God of the Israelites was a God not only for the Hebrews and the Jews, but for all people who would worship the Almighty and follow the Lord's ways."

"Awesome! I had no idea!" Bethany said as she laid back on the gold floor with her hands behind her head to better enjoy the glimmering gold carvings of the archangels near the top of the ceiling walls of the Temple. It was hard for her to take it all in – the beauty of the Temple, where she was, who she was with, what she was learning. Suddenly, rolling over on her side and supporting her head on one elbow, she said, "Hey Gabriel, you said there was one more woman … Esther. What did she do?"

"Oh, she was a sharp one. A real … 'rad' lady, I guess you could say. She became the Queen of all Persia. Her name meant 'star' and she certainly was one, as much as any actress in Hollywood. And was she cool under pressure! Able to turn the tables on her enemy, that lady could!"

"When did she live?"

"Oh, let's see … Ezra, Nehemiah, and *Esther* – the last three books of History – all cover roughly the same period. That is … during the return from the 'exile' … during the period of the rebuilding of the Temple and its walls, which was about 500 B.C."

Bethany quickly got up on her knees and looked straight at Gabriel. "You mean this Temple? This beautiful Temple was destroyed? And what do you mean about the period of the exile?"

"I thought we covered that," Gabriel said, scratching his chin. "Well, anyway," Gabriel went on, "maybe the best way to explain the exile is to go back to the days just following the death of Solomon – that is, the final days of the united kingdom of Israel. You see, Bethany, I guess it's fair to say that David was the King of Israel who, more than any other, fought to expand its territory. On the other hand, his son, Solomon, was a builder, not a fighter, and he was in many ways 'wise,' especially when it came to making business contacts and political alliances. Yes, Solomon was what you call … one shrewd dude! You see, King David had conquered territory that included important trade routes linking Egypt, Asia, Arabia, Asia Minor, and Syria. Solomon figured out that if these traders from other countries could be guaranteed peaceful passage through his land, they would be willing to pay Israel something for it. And he could use this extra money to help his building programs, which were his first love."

"Oh, I get it. He would charge a tariff or tax, right?" Bethany said, recalling her social studies lesson on this subject weeks before at school. "You know, my uncle always says that some foreign countries are flooding our country with goods, and we should raise our import tax on them since they won't let a lot of our goods into their country. How did the foreign countries handle those taxes back then? Would they let Israel's goods into their country?"

"Bethany, I really don't know about that. But you do bring up a good point – politics. Solomon was a master politician. For example, when he wanted to build the Temple and to use cedar and cypress wood for a great deal of the Temple interior, he turned to the foreign King of Tyre."

"Why did he do that? Didn't Israel have the wood?"

"Not the best kind. Tyre, a town in present day Lebanon, had that. And so Solomon made a deal with King Hiram to supply it. And he made other what I will call 'political deals' to secure what he believed would bring peace and prosperity to Israel. For example, he married a Moabite, an Ammonite, an Edomite and an Egyptian, a daughter of the Pharaoh. He probably figured no country would attack his country if he was the son-in-law of that people's leader."

"Did he have any Hebrew wives?"

"Oh, yes, quite a few."

"How many?"

"I'm not sure how many were Hebrew and how many were foreign, but the Bible tells us he had seven hundred in all," Gabriel commented.

"Seven hundred! Seven hundred! You're not serious!"

"Very serious. First Kings 11:3, I'm fairly certain. Although, I agree it seems quite excessive."

"Excessive? I think it's downright ridiculous! How could he even remember all their names?"

After a moment, a broad smirk came across Gabriel's face, as he responded, "Name tags?" And then he began to chuckle.

"That's not very funny! He had more wives than some towns have people!"

"OK. OK, you're right, Bethany," Gabriel acknowledged, as he got back to his story. "And God and the Israelite people weren't very happy about it either. These 'marriages for convenience' were turning Solomon away from his one and only God, for many of his foreign wives continued to worship their own gods. Besides that, can you imagine the size of the King's palace complex to house all of these women? It took thirteen years just to build it – six years longer than it took to build the Temple to God Almighty! Plus, the tribes were being taxed heavily and were forced to work on these building projects without pay! Can you imagine!"

"That's unfair! I wouldn't do it. No way, José!" Bethany responded, with a determined frown on her face.

"That's an interesting expression. Who is José? And where did you learn that one?"

"Oh, it's been around for awhile. My father told me how it got started. José was this guy who used to go to all the home town baseball games – a real regular. He never missed a game! It would rain; he'd be there. It was boiling hot; he was there. José would always cheer for the team – win or lose – he'd make them feel important. When the team was way behind, he'd say things like 'Don't give up; you can do it! You can come back! There's enough time!' Or if they lost, he'd say 'Don't worry, you'll be back; you'll get them next time!' You see, my dad says that a team is only as good as the fans that stand behind them. And if the fans stink, the team's likely going to stink too. Anyway, the team had done well until a September slump when they lost nine in a row, and this last game would decide whether they would play for the pennant. It was the bottom of the ninth, two outs, and the bases were loaded. The home team's worst hitter was at the plate, with his team trailing by three runs. It would take a miracle to win it."

"Oh, my!" Gabriel interjected.

"The batter was sweating bullets. It was his first year in the major leagues, and he was having problems getting used to playing with the 'big boys.' His batting average wasn't great, and he hadn't hit a home run all year. Well, when he realized that José, his favorite fan, wasn't cheering for him, he felt hopeless. The most important play in the game, and José was nowhere to be found!"

"What did the batter do?"

"Well, the rookie batter said to the coach 'there's no way José would leave this game. We've got to find him.' The team was going to page José on the ball park's sound system, but it had broken two innings before. So finally, the batter asked the big lady in the front row if she had a loud voice. She said she had studied opera or something and that she could out shout anyone in the stadium. Well, things were getting crazy – all the fans were yelling and the other team insisted the batter step up to the plate or forfeit the game."

"Oh, this is exciting! What happened next?"

"The batter said, 'Hey lady, ask José if he can see the game.' And she yelled out in a voice that sounded something like singing 'José can you see?' It was so loud José heard her, came running back to his seat, and began to cheer as always. The batter was so happy that he stepped up to the plate. On the very next throw, he hit the ball out of the park by a good twenty feet – winning the game! And that's why we sing the Star Spangled Banner at all baseball games today because the first line sounds like 'José, can you see?' It reminds us of the importance of our country *and* of being a good fan!"

"Oh, I see. Very interesting," Gabriel remarked, not sure whether this was a story he should believe. It did seem somewhat logical, however. After a moment of reflection, Gabriel had to ask, "One thing I don't understand, why did José leave in the first place, if he was such a big fan?"

Bethany at first shrugged her shoulders, but then her eyes twinkled as she said, "Bathroom break?"

Gabriel smirked at Bethany's comment and then said, "Speaking of breaks, let's go somewhere different. You know, you have been training hard. Let's go to a mountain in the north of Israel near the Mediterranean Ocean to witness one of the most exciting events in the Bible. I'll tell you more when we get there." Gabriel held out his hand to Bethany and, as she and Oba stood by the angel's side, they were transported to the mountain by the sea.

Chapter 17
A Faint Light Remains

Bethany viewed the "Great Sea" from atop the mountain. It was a superb view. The ocean had a blue haze that matched the sky, so much so that it was hard to tell where one stopped and the other started. In the distance she saw hundreds of people in flowing robes who appeared to be of royalty walking toward the peak of the mountain.

"Gabriel, where are we and who are all those people coming up here?"

"Oh, this is going to be special, Bethany. You'll see. It's really, really cool. We're on Mount Carmel, and we're about to experience an incredible contest."

"Mount Carmel? They should have called it Mount Camel 'cause we're on a big hump here – aren't we? Anyway, who is that old geezer over there who is dressed in those rags. He's all by himself. Doesn't he have any friends?"

"Bethany, he doesn't have many friends here, but he's got the best one you can have. You see, that's Elijah – one of the greatest Prophets in the Bible."

"Elijah, I don't remember anything about him. What did he do?"

"You haven't read much of the first book of Kings have you? Don't worry. We'll cover that shortly. Listen, while the audience is getting here, let me set this up for you so you'll know what's going on. But stay with my story so you'll understand how important this event is. OK?"

"OK, Coach. Fire when ready," Bethany said as she let Oba go to exercise his body while she listened.

"Now, Bethany, as I was saying earlier, God was upset with Solomon for marrying all those foreign women and allowing them to worship other gods. God told Solomon that he had broken his covenant, err ... his family's agreement, not to worship or let others worship other gods. For this violation, God was going to, after Solomon's death, tear away a large portion of his kingdom and God gave it to Jeroboam, who was an Ephraimite; that is, a person from the tribe of Ephraim. But because of God's great love for David, God would leave the tribe of Judah in the hands of David's grandson, whose name was Rehoboam. And God, speaking through one of his Prophets, told this to Jeroboam also, saying, beginning with First Kings 11:36:

> Yet to [Solomon's] son I will give one tribe, so that my servant David may always have a lamp before me in Jerusalem, the city where I have chosen to put my name. I will take [Jeroboam], and you shall reign over all that your soul desires, you shall be king over Israel. If you will listen to all that I command you, walk in my ways, and do what is right in my sight by keeping my statutes and my commandments, as David my servant did, I will be with you, and will build you an enduring house, as I built for David, and I will give Israel to you. For this

reason I will punish the descendants of
David, but not forever."

"Wow!" Bethany said. "So Solomon had all of Israel
and because he broke God's covenant, God ripped it all
away from his tribe, except the land of Judah. What a
bummer!"

"A bummer, indeed! Anyway, after Solomon's death,
Israel was split in two. One part was Israel, consisting of the
northern tribes – ruled by the tribe of Ephraim. The other
part was Judah – ruled, of course, by the tribe of Judah. It
also appears that Judah incorporated the land just north of
it as a kind of 'buffer' or 'protection' against the other
tribes. This was the property of the tribe of Benjamin, and
it's not clear if Judah got this buffer property by an alliance
with Benjamin or by brute force. Anyway, as you can
imagine, the northern and southern tribes began to fight
each other for territory. Rather like your War Between the
States, I imagine. And, as a divided kingdom, they were
more vulnerable ... err ... more easily attacked by their
enemies."

Bethany nodded at Gabriel confirming that this
information had sunk in, but, out of the corner of her eye,
she was also watching the antics of Oba, who as always was
trying another trick. This one involved leaping up on top
of a large rock over five feet in height and then doing a flip
forward in the air and landing on the other side of the
boulder on all fours. Bethany thought he would have made
a great gymnast and that the pummel horse would have
been one of his favorite events.

"Well, anyway," Gabriel continued, "unfortunately,
Jeroboam didn't listen to God any more than Solomon did
during the last years of his life. Jeroboam established the
town of Shechem, in the land of Ephraim, as the capital of
Israel and almost immediately began worshiping idols of
other gods. Later, the capital was moved even further north
to a town called Samaria which is still pretty far south from

here. Anyway, the kings of Judah didn't do a whole lot better, although there were a few good kings interspersed with the bad ones. And that's where all the Prophets come in."

"The Prophets?"

"Yes, the Prophets. You know, the Law, the History, and the Prophets!" Gabriel said with emphasis.

"Oh, yes. I remember."

"Here, let's look at the books of the Prophets," Gabriel said as he pulled out a list from his back pocket and unfolded it carefully.

MAJOR	MINOR	
Isaiah	Hosea	Preached during northern
	Joel	kingdom period
	Amos	(Before 722 B.C.)
	Obadiah	
	Jonah	
	Micah	
Jeremiah	Nahum	Preached after fall
Lamentations	Habakkuk	of northern kingdom
Ezekiel	Zephaniah	(After 722 B.C.)
Daniel		
	Haggai	Preached after return
	Zechariah	to Jerusalem (Post-Exile
	Malachi	Period) (After 538 B.C.)

"As you can see, those who compiled the Bible placed these books in order of the time in which they believed the Prophets lived. However, a number of Bible scholars believe that some of these books, including Joel, Obadiah, Jonah and Daniel, may not be in the correct order, but this order should be acceptable for your competition."

"OK. But, you know, I don't see Elijah anywhere. You told me he was a great Prophet. What happened to him?"

"Elijah was one of the earliest Prophets – so early that his stories are covered in the History of the Kings rather than under the books of the Prophets. Anyway, the Prophets, including Elijah, tried to tell the kings of the northern kingdom of Israel and the southern kingdom of Judah that if they and their people didn't change their ways and go back to the ways of the Lord, they would be handed over to their enemies. And Elijah was the Prophet who was in one of the most celebrated contests in the Old Testament."

"What kind of contest?"

"It was God against Baal, the Canaanite or Phoenician god, who was supposed to control the rain," Gabriel remarked. "You see, Ahab was the Israelite king of the northern kingdom who married a Canaanite woman named Jezebel. This woman was about as wicked and dominating a queen as there ever was. She was bound and determined to convert her husband, Ahab, and the Israelites in the northern kingdom to Baalism, her religion. In fact, I think I see her coming up the mountain now. See that woman over there with the stunning robe and her neck and arms covered with jewels. That's Jezebel all right. She's pretty decked out, isn't she?"

"Well, yes, she is, but why on earth did Ahab marry her in the first place?" Bethany inquired. "I don't think she's that pretty."

"Politics. Just like Solomon, he wanted to have an alliance with her father who was the king of Sidon, a city in Phoenicia … err … present day Lebanon. This was so that when Ahab had to fight the Syrians to the north he could count on the people of Sidon for help."

"The Syrians? You mean like the country of Syria?"

"That's right."

"Boy! The Jewish people have found it hard to get

along with their neighbors for a long time! As my dad always says when people don't get along, 'someone forgot to read Carnegie!'"

"Andrew Carnegie, the American philanthropist?" Gabriel inquired, not understanding the significance of this statement.

"No," Bethany said, cocking her head to one side, "it was probably his sister or something. Her name was Dale."

"Oh … well, anyway," Gabriel said, once again continuing his story, "Elijah forecasted a long drought which was to last for years in order to punish Ahab for permitting the Baal practices of Jezebel. In the meantime, Jezebel persuaded her husband to start killing these Prophets of God, and Elijah hid for several years before God said it was time for a show-down at the OK Corral!"

"Huh? What's the OK Corral?" Bethany said, looking rather puzzled.

"It's this place in a great old western movie where …" Gabriel then realized that they had other information to cover. "Never mind! Let's just say that God said it was time to prove that his power was greater than that of any other gods. So he had Elijah challenge the prophets of Baal to a contest to see who was more powerful. And this event is going to take place shortly right here on this mountain!"

"Oh, man, this is like major, major awesome! Hey Gabriel, what are they placing on those two altars?"

"The meat of bulls for the offerings: one for Baal and one for God. And underneath the offering is wood for burning. But Elijah has a challenge to the priests. Let's listen. I believe Elijah is going to speak."

Elijah raised his hands to silence the crowd before he spoke. "For many years now, the Israelite people have turned their hearts from the Lord, and you, King Ahab, have dishonored God in the most insulting manner, by the worship of a false god – the god of Baal – the Canaanite god. Your true God and the one and only God has sent me to tell you that the terrible drought in Israel over the past few years has been caused by your actions. And God will prove to you today that the hundreds of Canaanite prophets and the god of Baal are no match for a single Prophet who comes in the name of the true God. Now, tell your god to light the wood for the offering to Baal." Elijah then calmly waited.

It was quite a sight: over eight hundred Canaanite prophets jumping up and down, praying and pleading, trying to get their false god to light that fire, but they couldn't do it! Not even a spark! Covering her mouth, Bethany couldn't help but laugh at the comical wailing and gyrating prophets of Baal.

When these prophets became exhausted, Elijah spoke up and said, "Pour water over my altar to the Lord. Get the wood good and wet." The men complied.

"Gabriel, what is he doing?"

"Do it again," Elijah said. Once again the wood was saturated with water.

"Is he crazy?" Bethany said quietly as she leaned over and looked at Gabriel again. Gabriel just grinned.

"One final time," Elijah yelled with a strong voice so all could hear. Everyone was standing around quite amazed at Elijah's confidence. Finally, Elijah called out to the Lord to light the wood and, in an instant, the wood burst into huge flames and consumed the offering! The prophets of Baal were awestruck by what they were observing and at least momentarily were silent as they turned and began to file down the mountain, defeated by a single Prophet of God.

As Bethany watched the entourage of people descending the mountain, Bethany commented, "Wow! That was some contest! God hit a home run, and Baal didn't get to first base! Coach, didn't Ahab begin to follow God's ways after that?"

"Believe it or not, just for a short period. Then Jezebel convinced Ahab that it was just a trick, and he went back to

Baal worship. You know, it was a continual battle for the Prophets to try to turn the kings around to the ways of the Lord. Some kings were not as bad as others but the bottom line was that God eventually punished his chosen people by allowing both the northern and southern kingdom to be overrun by their enemies. The northern kingdom fell first – into the hands of the Assyrians in 722 B.C. They took most of the tribes of the northern kingdom and spread them all around Assyria's other conquered cities. These tribes were so dispersed that, as a family, they never got back to Israel in significant numbers and were thereafter known as the 'lost tribes of Israel.'"

"Boy! That's sad!" Bethany exclaimed. "Joseph would have been very disappointed that his family got split up like that. What about Judah?"

"Judah lasted for well over another hundred years but, in 586 B.C., Judah was defeated by the Babylonians, who, by the way, had also defeated the Assyrians. Incidentally, the Babylonians were also known as the Chaldeans or Neo-Babylonians. Anyway, it was at this time that they destroyed the Temple in Jerusalem."

"What happened to the people of Judah?" Bethany commented with concern in her voice.

"The 'Jews,' who get their name from their tribe of Judah, were carried to the city of Babylon, where they reflected on the good old days in Jerusalem and began to write down their history in books – some of which were to become part of the Old Testament. Fortunately, many of the Jews did eventually get back to Jerusalem."

"How long before they returned?"

"About seventy years in all to get back and rebuild the temple." Gabriel reported. "The cruel King Nebuchadnezzar II of Babylonia was in charge of them initially during their exile."

"Oh! I remember him," she said quoting the following

verse: 'Nebuchadnezzar, King of the Jews, can you spell that without any 'u's?''

Gabriel hesitated for a moment not knowing what to make of this rhyme, but finally said, "No, I don't believe I can."

Bethany, with a satisfied look on her face, enunciated the letters slowly "T ... H ... A ... T! The word 'THAT' has no u's!" she giggled and then covered her mouth with her hand, as Gabriel looked at her unapprovingly with a slight frown.

"Bethany, it's not nice to fool your teacher! Besides, that riddle is misleading. Nebuchadnezzar was king of the Babylonians and conqueror of the Jews." Slowly, his frown turned into a grin as he went on, "Although I must say it is silly enough to make you remember his name. And that may be important for your contest! Anyway, this period where the Jews were in Babylon is referred to as the period of the 'exile.' Later, after the Babylonians had been defeated by the Persians, Cyrus the Great from Persia allowed the Jews to return to Jerusalem to rebuild the Temple and the walls of the city."

"The Persians? That's Iran today, isn't it? And the Babylonians are the people of Iraq. Right?"

"Correct on both counts!" Gabriel confirmed. "Well, anyway, the Prophets are organized in order based on whether they were preaching before the fall of the northern kingdom or after its fall. Remember we are talking about *time* here and not whether a Prophet preached to the people of the northern kingdom or to the people of the southern kingdom."

"Isaiah is listed first among the Major Prophets and he is the only Major Prophet who preached during the *time period* that the northern kingdom (Israel) existed. Jeremiah (and his Lamentations) and Ezekiel were preaching during the period after the fall of the northern kingdom. So, obviously, they were telling the southern kingdom – Judah

– to repent and change its ways or meet the same fate as the lost tribes of Israel."

"What about Daniel? He was one of my favorites. You know, the lions' den and all that." Bethany was trying to absorb all that her coach was saying but was having trouble since Oba really wanted to play and kept jumping up in the air to get her attention. Bethany decided, while still listening to Gabriel, to try and teach Oba to leap over a stick that she held horizontally in the air – multi-tasking she liked to call it. Within a few minutes, Obadiah was performing well and could leap over the stick at heights that Bethany could not believe. "This animal is extremely smart and incredibly athletic – no question about it," she thought to herself as she continued to listen to Gabriel.

Gabriel, observing the doggie tricks, was impressed but decided not to comment and instead continued with his lesson. "Daniel is even later, since he was a Prophet that is reported to have lived during the Jews' exile in Babylon as was the case with the Major Prophet, Ezekiel. So don't forget that."

"I'll try not to, Gabriel."

On top of Mount Carmel with its stunning view of the area, Gabriel and Bethany spent time studying the Major and Minor Prophets. Gabriel attempted to answer all her questions. One question was of special interest to Bethany because of her dog, Oba. "Gabriel, the Minor Prophet Obadiah, what did he say in his book?"

"I'm glad you asked. I guess you should know since your canine companion is named for him. Say, we need to get back to the Temple. Something strange was going on when we left, and I want to check it out. When we get there, why don't you take a few minutes and read the entire book of Obadiah. It's the shortest book in the Old Testament – just a couple of pages really. And while you read it, I'll whip up a glorious datenut shake for your culinary delight. That would be especially appropriate in light of your name."

"That would be great, I think. You know, I've never had a datenut shake before, so this will be interesting. Hey, why did you say that it was so appropriate?"

"Child, I will fill you in on that one after you try it! Now grab Oba and stand next to me." In a flash they were once again transported back to the Temple.

Chapter 18
Datenut Shake

Gabriel noticed, with some concern, that almost all the merchants had left the Temple area outside, even though the market area was usually open for a few more hours. He prepared Bethany's datenut shake as promised and handed it to her to drink. While studying her lesson, she had a few sips, and said, "Gabriel this is pretty good. Now can you tell me about this drink?"

"OK, but you may be a bit embarrassed by what I am going to tell you."

"Try me."

"You obviously don't even know what your own name means."

"Oh, man, I can't believe it. Gabriel, I've got a lot to learn, don't I? This is embarrassing. You mean I'm named after a milkshake flavor?"

Gabriel tried not to laugh. "Hardly. You see your name has Hebrew origins. 'Beth' in Hebrew means 'house' and 'Bethany' means 'house of dates.' As a fruit, dates were an important source of nourishment to the people of Israel. So you have a good biblical name – that's for sure."

"You know, Gabriel, just when I begin to think I know a lot, I find out just how dumb I am," Bethany said, her ego deflated.

"Don't be so hard on yourself, Bethany. Lots of people much older than you don't know the meaning of their names. But the Hebrew people thought what a person's name meant was very important. We all have areas where our knowledge is lacking. But you have learned a great deal in a short period and you will learn much more! Now what did you think of your old buddy Obadiah? What was he preaching about?"

"It was kind of strange to me. It looked like he was all upset with the Edomites. They hadn't been very nice to the Israelites, and like he was saying to those mean people that they were going to be sorry!"

"Well, you might say it that way. You know, we don't know much about Obadiah. On the other hand, we do know that the Edomites were descendants of Esau – you know, Jacob's brother – and they lived in the hills near the southeast corner of the Salt Sea, later called the Dead Sea. Basically, they were just around the corner from Judah. Judah was attacked and defeated by the Babylonians in 586 B.C. and carried away to live in exile in Babylon. And it appears that the Edomites even helped the Babylonians defeat Judah. Now, if Obadiah was with the Jews of Judah during this sad period, it wouldn't surprise me that he would have been furious that Jacob's cousins had 'sold them down the river,' so to speak."

"Gee, Gabriel, why didn't they stick together, being cousins and all."

"I see your point. But remember, this strained relationship goes all the way back to the fight between Jacob and Esau over the birthright from their father, Isaac. Plus, later the Edomites wouldn't even let Moses and his people, on their way to the Promised Land, travel through their property, even though Moses had agreed to pay for any damages caused by their passage. This made the Israelites very angry."

"That's terrible," Bethany responded. "When things get tough, you sure find out who your friends are!" Suddenly, Oba ran up to Bethany and kept jumping across her lap as if to say, "I'm here! I'm here! Let's play!" Bethany patted his head as she continued, "Hey, Gabriel, speaking of friends, what did you say Obadiah's name meant?"

"It means 'God's servant.' Why?"

"Oh, that's cool, 'cause I think he's going to help us serve God in some special way."

"Sounds good to me! What do you think, Oba?" Oba began to prance around, leaping up and down and bobbing his head from side to side, because of the attention.

Suddenly Gabriel remembered, "Oh, there is another thing you should remember to help you in the contest."

"What's that?" Bethany asked, hoping to avoid any curve ball a judge might throw her.

"Do you remember that earlier you asked me about Esther? And I said that the last three books of History – Ezra, Nehemiah and Esther, all cover about the same period of time. That is, they cover the period of the Jews' return to Jerusalem from the exile, which was about 500 to 400 B.C."

"Yes. And I remember that your chart shows Nehemiah as 500 B.C."

"Well, the last three books of the Minor Prophets are the same. That is, Haggai, Zechariah and Malachi were all about that same period: the period where the Jews were allowed to leave Babylon and return to Jerusalem to rebuild the Temple. So if the judges ask you a question about which book talks about something happening during the rebuilding of the Temple, you can narrow it down to six books fairly easily. And if it's a Prophet question, you're probably down to three. Get it?"

"Got it! Wow! That's a good tip, Coach!" Bethany said with great excitement in her voice.

"You know," Gabriel continued, "there is at least one more Prophet that you should be aware of who lived during the period of the northern kingdom. He was Elisha. The Prophet Elijah had hand picked Elisha as his successor – the one to follow him. They were the most powerful Prophets from the time of Samuel to the time of Isaiah. Want to take a guess at when they lived?"

"Well," Bethany started, "I remember that Samuel picked Saul and David as kings and that David lived about 1000 B.C." She then reviewed the "Super Seven" chart that Gabriel had created, giving major dates and events.

"And I see that Isaiah was about 700 B.C., so it obviously was between that period."

"Good!" Gabriel said, pleased. "Now remember, all you have to do for the contest is be within 100 years of the right date, so make sure you 'hedge your bet.'"

"I'm not sure what you mean by 'hedge,' but I know that you of all ... err ... people shouldn't be recommending to a child that she should bet. I mean my mom says that betting is usually a sinful activity, where one person takes another person's money based upon some silly event that has nothing to do with intelligence or need or anything like that. And that those who really need their money are the ones who are going to bet the most and lose it. But, you know, my Uncle Lot disagrees with her."

"Why am I not surprised?" Gabriel remarked, under his breath.

"Yes. You see, my uncle says that the whole foundation of our capitalistic system is based on betting."

"It is?" Gabriel said, quite intrigued by this statement.

"Uh-huh. He says that capitalism depends on risk taking and that the more risk a person takes the more reward he should possibly receive. And that's why he thinks that state lotteries are a good idea."

"He does, does he?"

"Yeah, my uncle says that these lotteries teach us a

valuable lesson – some people are lucky and some aren't, and if you're thinking about going into business for yourself, it helps to have not only 'smarts' but some luck, too. That's the risk a businessman takes anytime he starts out on his own."

"Oh, does your uncle have his own business?" Gabriel inquired.

"Well, he used to and that's why he knows so much about these things. Plus, he says this is obvious if you think about it. Look at Harvard University, for example. He says they graduate some of the smartest, most educated people in the world, and yet some of their alumni aren't rich and some aren't even financially secure, mainly because they just plain didn't have good luck. Anyway, my uncle says some people have lots less smarts but much more good luck, and they come out financially ahead. And that's the importance of the lottery: to remind us all that some people are smart and some people are lucky, and they aren't necessarily the same people. And capitalism is the system that allows even the not-so-smart, lucky people to get rich, if they're willing to take a chance. He says bingo reminds us of this, but in a small way. What do you think?"

"Well," Gabriel rolled his eyes and scratched his chin as he thought. "I believe that some people at Harvard and elsewhere might not be rich or even 'financially secure,' as you put it, because their goal in life is not to make a lot of money or collect material things. Maybe their goal is to help others."

"That's what my mom says."

"Well, anyway, back to my point," Gabriel continued. "What was my point?" he said a little embarrassed with his inability to recall.

"You were talking about hedging your bets."

"Oh, yes! Now I remember," Gabriel said, delighted with Bethany's cue. "Let me give you an example. Now you told me that Elijah and Elisha must have lived between

1000 B.C. and 700 B.C. So if you didn't know the answer and had to guess, the best thing to do is pick a date right down the middle or split the difference."

"Oh, you mean pick a date in the middle like ... 850 B.C.?"

"Precisely! And since these men lived around 900 to 800 B.C., you would be in the money ... err ... I mean, you would be correct. Now, remember, that these two men were quite different personalities. Based on your observations at Mount Carmel, I guess you can recall that Elijah was a real Prophet of judgment and severity. There was no gray area between right and wrong. If you broke God's law, he'd tell you pretty quickly that you would be punished and that was that. On the other hand, Elisha was more of a Prophet promoting love and forgiveness," Gabriel concluded. "Although even Elisha had moments where his actions were quite severe. Both of these Prophets' stories are covered in the books of Kings. Let me pick out a few good chapters for you to read."

After reading the passages that Gabriel had selected, Bethany remarked, "You know, they were so different, but I know I'm going to forget who came first. Their names are so similar that it's confusing," Bethany replied, hoping Gabriel would give her another pointer on how to keep them straight.

"Actually, the similarity of, and one distinction in, their names make it easy to remember who came first. For example, what's the only letters in their names that are different?"

Bethany thought this one over for a moment and replied, "Elijah has a 'j' in it and Elisha has an 's.'"

"Correct! And logically, if you know the alphabet, you know which came first."

"Oh! I get it. The letter 'j' comes before 's,' so Elijah came first. Right?"

"Right! Another way to remember their order is to call them what I call them – the 'Ah-Ha!' Prophets."

"What?" Bethany couldn't quite understand.

"Ah-Ha!: That's the ending of Elijah and Elisha, in that order."

"Oh, I see now. Ah-Ha! I like that one."

Bethany stood up to stretch, as she looked around the Temple. Suddenly, a roaring noise arose throughout the streets – sounds of men fighting and swords clashing as they fought. The clamor grew louder and louder. Oba trembled with fright and then jumped into Bethany's arms. Bethany, holding the shivering canine tightly, turned to Gabriel and yelled, "Gabriel, what's going on?"

In a moment, soldiers entered the Temple and began to grab the gold ornaments that were not affixed to the floors or walls and broke into the store rooms, taking all the valuables that they could carry away. "It's the Babylonians!" Gabriel yelled. "Stand close. Let's get out of here!" he exclaimed as he nervously began to adjust the JOY device.

"Wait!" Bethany said. "They're destroying the Temple. We've got to stop them," as she tripped with her foot one of the passing soldiers who then stumbled and fell to the floor. He quickly jumped up perplexed by what had happened and, then looking in Bethany's direction, let out a yell, throwing the gold candlesticks in his hands to the floor and running from the Temple.

Bethany, surprised, asked Gabriel, "Gabriel, do I look that bad? Why was the soldier afraid of me?"

"He wasn't afraid of you! He couldn't even see you! All he saw was your dog floating through the air. You see, generally, only God can have us appear to people in the past. Otherwise, they can't see us. On the other hand, as you have discovered, animals can be seen quite well."

"Great! Then we'll be able to defend the Temple," she said, as she ran and tripped another Babylonian soldier who, upon seeing the small, growling dog in mid-air, began jumping around, waiving his hands, and screaming as if he had seen a mischievous spirit come to life. "Gabriel, help me. We must save this beautiful Temple and the Ark of the Covenant from destruction." Grabbing and unfolding Moses' rod given to her by Gabriel, Bethany whacked the legs of another incoming soldier who lost his balance and began to fall. She then held the yelping dog high above her head, while the soldier stumbled backwards and fell twice as he retreated out the Temple. Bethany repeated this process several times – striking each entering soldier's legs with her rod and then holding up Oba to frighten him. Next she took out her replica of David's sling and some small stones from the case where the sling had been kept. The Mighty Mustard Seed began hurling the rocks at the soldiers, hitting several in the head. Observing their companions lying unconscious on the floor by the nuggets thrown from the sling, the incoming soldiers sought safety behind a large pillar in the Temple.

Finally, Gabriel yelled, "Bethany, it's not our job to change history! Let's go! It's time for another test," he said, grabbing Bethany and her dog, as they attempted to defend the Temple. In an instant, with the help of JOY, they were transported to their new venue.

Chapter 19
Brahma Bull Barreling Contest

When Bethany's eyes cleared, she realized that she was in a small, dusty village. At first she was upset with Gabriel for transporting them away from the Temple, but she finally began to understand that for them to interfere with history was inappropriate and dangerous.

Bethany had a few questions regarding her new location and what was going on. "Coach, where are we, and why have we come here?"

"Oh, we're in that little town called Bethlehem for the big event! You know, your contest! Isn't this going to be cool!" Gabriel commented as he watched the other contestants stroll through the village area. "The preliminary rounds will be held in those small huts over there," he said as he pointed to the area.

"Will you be able to help me, Gabriel?"

"Not during the actual competition. However, I can assist you between rounds, and I'll always be there for moral support."

"Gabriel, I don't know about this. I didn't think it would be this soon."

"Oh, you'll do just fine. Pretty exciting isn't it? People

from all over the world and all walks of life are in this competition. It's just so grand to finally be here!"

*　　*　　*　　*　　*　　*　　*

While some of the questions were tough, Bethany breezed through the first seven rounds answering most of them with great confidence, given her knowledge of the Super Seven list and her superior training with Gabriel. Interestingly, each round had a different slant: some rounds focused on a "multiple choice" format while others mixed "question and answers" with "essays." She won one round based on her ability to write the best poem incorporating biblical references. All Gabriel's cross training had paid off, although she had yet to use her physical training and the rod and sling that Gabriel had given her.

In the eighth round, the competition was down to some incredibly knowledgeable contestants. As Bethany stood in front of her judge with her hands sweating, she realized that she had already answered almost twenty questions correctly for this round. She believed that if she got a few more correct she would definitely advance to the next round. It would be close, however, since most of the contestants at this level had not missed a single question. Finally, the judge asked Bethany her next question, "Miss, explain to me how Joseph, the son of Jacob, got to Egypt?"

Bethany went into great detail about his relationship with his jealous brothers, and concluded by saying, "... and Joseph was taken there by traders after his brothers sold him into slavery."

"Correct!" the judge confirmed. "Now, another question: name two reasons why Ruth was important and the time period in which she lived."

Bethany was excited about this question since she and Gabriel had discussed it in detail, but she considered her answer carefully before responding. "She was a Moabite – a non-Israelite – who was loyal to God, and this showed that God was here for *all* people." Bethany then continued, "She was also important because she was the great grandmother of King David of the tribe of Judah – the tribe of Jesus' family."

"Correct on both counts!" said the judge. "And when did she live?"

Bethany contemplated for a moment about the Super Seven list and when David lived, and finally commented, "Ruth lived about 1100 to 1000 B.C., probably 1050 B.C." (She had remembered to "split the difference" when she wasn't sure, just as Gabriel had told her to do.)

"Very good. That is an acceptable answer." The judge then looked at Bethany and said, "Please answer the following three-part question: first, who came first – Elij*ah* or Elis*ha?*; second, how many days did Elijah travel in the desert going to Mount Horeb?; and, third, what was the other name for this mountain?"

Remembering Gabriel's memory aid "Ah-Ha," Bethany answered, "Elijah came before Elisha." After a slight pause she continued, "And the other name for Mount Horeb is … is … Mt. Sinai."

"Correct on both parts!" said the judge with approval. "Now how about the number of days Elijah traveled in the desert to reach Mount Horeb? Be very careful with your answer, since I must tell you that your answer will decide whether you go to the next level – the Super Semi-Finals!"

Bethany's eyes lit up as she considered how incredible it would be to get to the Super Semi-Finals – one step closer to the Bible Bowl Championship! Yet, her hope sank when she realized that she didn't have a clue! Gabriel had failed to cover this question. Her hands fidgeted with her hair as she tried to perform macro-association and think "big picture." First she thought of what would be some good biblical numbers based on what she and Gabriel had discussed. Twelve was good: the twelve tribes, the twelve disciples, the twelve days of Christmas. Of course, ten was good: the Ten Commandments, the ten plagues against Egypt. Seven was also good: God created the earth in seven days. What about forty? she thought: Noah and the flood lasted forty days and nights; Moses spent forty days on Mount Sinai getting instructions from God – and he and the Israelite people wandered in the desert for forty years.

"Come now, young lady. We must have an answer."

She lowered her head and prayed a moment, hoping this would clear her mind and allow her to remember some helpful information. And then she actually recalled something she had learned from Sunday school many months before. Jesus wandered in the desert for forty days while being tempted by the devil. In her mind she began to see a possible pattern: the number forty seemed to have a connection with major testing, training and cleansing periods in the desert. She couldn't be sure, but forty seemed as good a guess as any. Finally she said with trepidation in her voice, "Is the answer forty, forty days in the desert?"

"Young lady," the judge said slowly, "I'm sorry to inform you that you won't ..." (Bethany's heart begin to crumble.) "... be going home for a few more days – *'cause you've made it to the Super Semi-Finals!"*

Gabriel was just outside the small hut and overhearing the announcement, he grabbed Oba and impulsively threw him high into the air and was ready to catch him on the way down. Oba, twisting his torso in mid-air, did a flip and landed comfortably on all fours on the low-hanging roof. Sensing the excitement, Obadiah began to howl with joy. The judges laughed at the dog's actions, while applauding Bethany's fine performance. A small ceremony was held outside the hut, honoring her accomplishment.

* * * * * * *

Bethany worked hard with Gabriel every chance she got. She knew that a win at this level would put her in the championship round – The Super Bible Bowl! Finally the day of the contest arrived. For the first time, the competition was going to be in an outdoor arena – located only a few miles outside the Bethlehem village. The size of the crowd was anticipated to be in the tens of thousands. Gabriel tried to prepare her for the tension and excitement of the next level of competition. Entering the coliseum filled to capacity, she was greeted with a large portion of the crowd cheering her name: "Beth-a-ny! Beth-a-ny! Beth-a-neee!"

Bethany couldn't believe her eyes and ears. Turning to Gabriel who entered by her side, she said, "Coach, what's this all about? How do they know my name? And why are they cheering for me?"

"I tried to prepare you for this. Everybody's been waiting for you. You're the youngest contestant. Plus, you've developed quite a reputation due to the way you handled yourself with the Old Woman I Know and your exploits in the Temple – you know, when you fought the Babylonians. That took courage, kiddo. Plus, frankly, you're kind of an underdog favorite. No one thought you could ever make it this far. There's some tough competition out there. But I know you can do it, Bethany. You're ready! Don't let anyone tell you that you're not!"

"Ladies and Gentlemen," said the announcer, "welcome to the First Annual, Super Semi-Final Bi—ble Booowl!!!! We will now announce the four contestants who will compete for the right to participate in the finals next week."

Bethany's stomach turned as the commentator announced the other three competitors. Each had developed such a reputation that she knew of them by their nicknames: "The Eliminator," a brilliant college professor from a major university whose specialty was dates and time periods and who had blown out all his prior opponents with his outstanding knowledge; "The Human Sponge," a well-known politician who had an uncanny ability to absorb thousands of people's names and little nuggets of information regarding their families; and "The Octopus," an exceptional genealogist who had spent over thirty years studying family trees, including his own and who had determined he was related by blood or marriage to approximately seventy percent of all known royalty in the world. Then there was Bethany – Bethany Anna Clarke. She was still working on the sixth grade and, until just recently, didn't even know what her own name meant – yet she was referred to by many as "The Mighty Mustard Seed."

Next the announcer presented the distinguished judges – twelve outstanding angels with impressive qualifications. As the judges stood to be recognized by the audience, Bethany noticed that they stared straight ahead with rather frustrated looks on their faces – only the head judge seemed to be smiling.

Bethany couldn't help but comment on her observation. "Gabriel, why aren't any of the judges smiling except the head judge?"

"Oh, rumor has it that these "super angels" have very big egos. Probably since they didn't get placed as the head judge, their feelings got hurt. I mean, angels are great on assignment when they are helping people, but when they get together, sometimes their competitive spirit won't let them let their halos down and enjoy each other's company. Anyway, they apparently aren't in a very good mood today."

Finally, as the crowd began to become fidgety, the announcer yelled, "Let the contest begin!"

Bethany looked at Gabriel and said, "Coach, I'm not feeling so hot. Can we come back tomorrow?"

"Nonsense child, you look fine. Now don't let these guys and their highbrow credentials throw you for a loop. Remember, you've had something they've never had."

"What's that?" Bethany inquired.

"Me as your coach!"

"Gabriel, you amaze me. Do you think you're that good?"

"No. But I think you are. Now get out there, partner, and get along little doggie!! Ya-hoooo!" He pointed toward the entrance of the coliseum as in ran four powerful western quarter horses, saddled and ready to ride. They kicked up a lot of dust before coming to an abrupt halt, as riders on other horses approached them from the other end of the coliseum. Gabriel was so excited he yelled, "It's Ro-de-o Time!" The crowd cheered as the horses were led over to the contestants.

Bethany shouted, "Gabriel, what's this all about?"

"Oh, I didn't get a chance to tell you. God announced it about ten minutes ago. The theme of the contest this year is 'Roundup for God.'"

"For a Bible contest?"

"Isn't God great! What a sense of humor! I mean, just when you think you have prepared for every contingency, in comes a curve ball like nobody's ready for. It sure makes the contest more realistic – like real life. And what fun!" Gabriel went on, as barrels were being set up at various locations within the coliseum. "This is going to be poppin'!!"

Bethany and the other contestants were dumbstruck in disbelief. The crowd went wild, loving the theme and eager for the contest to begin. As the master of ceremonies announced the rules, the events became clear: a barrel race, followed by calf roping, followed by Brahma bull barreling – undoubtedly the most exciting event for the viewing audience. In each of these three events, the contestants would be given a series of questions written on a piece of paper. They would be allowed to read the questions. That part of the contest was easy. Next, they must participate in the rodeo event, while reflecting on their answers, which were to be given to the judges after completion of the event. Points were given both for the best times and most correct answers.

Bethany became more and more excited as she put on her riding outfit, including her spurs and her cowboy hat. Someone in the crowd also gave her a red bandanna to tie around her neck for good luck. She felt confident about the first event: her riding lessons in Connecticut and her experiences in the desert on horseback with Gabriel should serve her well in the barrel race, she thought. She was a bit more uncomfortable with the calf roping since she had used a lasso only once – at a cousin's farm over a year ago. And the Brahma bull barreling sounded too bizarre for words. She decided not to worry about that one until later.

After the first two events, Bethany was in second place, behind the leader, The Eliminator. She learned that, as a young boy, he was raised on a farm and was good with horses and lassos. She was pleased with her oral answers – only missing two out of twenty. But her raw score for time and correct answers was way behind the leader. She was disappointed and worried that, with one event to go, she might not be able mathematically to surpass the Eliminator and win the contest. The Octopus was in last place – not because of his Bible knowledge – he had a perfect score in that area, but he had grown up in a large city and his horseback riding skills were unquestionably poor.

Bethany and Gabriel stood together waiting for the last event to be set up. It was early evening, and the contestants were tiring a bit. Unexpectedly, the master of ceremonies appeared and, in a booming voice, announced as he pointed to the sky, "Folks, we're pleased to announce that it's ... the ... 'Dai-ly Double!!!'" Momentarily, something similar to a roman candle streamed across the sky and the particles mysteriously spelled out the words "Daily Double." Dozens of clowns ran into the coliseum waving their arms, jumping up and down and doing cartwheels and back flips, to which the crowd responded with a roar of approval. Bethany looked toward the judges table and all twelve were smiling, pleased with the crowd's reaction. Continuing to howl and shout, the multitude was whipped into near pandemonium by the clowns' constant parading around and waving their hands in the air. Finally, the master of ceremonies approached the contestants to provide the rules for the last event.

"Now contestants, listen carefully. This third and final event of the day is a 'Daily Double,' which means your raw score of time and Bible answers will be worth twice as much as the other two events," the announcer said. (The Eliminator, as the leader, looked frustrated as he realized that this put all the other contestants back in the game. Of course, the other contestants, including Bethany, were gleeful at this last minute development.) "Your mission," he continued, "should you decide to accept it, is written on this piece of paper, along with a single question that you must answer on the back of the paper for the judges after completing the Brahma bull barreling event." As the contestants opened their papers to read the instructions, the clowns were preparing the field of play – placing large barrels all about – large enough for two people to get inside comfortably.

Bethany and Gabriel read the paper together – Objective: Put bull through barrel. Time Limit: 30 minutes. Question: What have you learned? Keep answer short.

Bethany and Gabriel both shook their heads in disbelief, as Bethany whispered, "Coach, that's impossible. Isn't it?"

Gabriel responded, "It will be difficult, no doubt. Those barrels are way too small. You must use all our resources on this one. I suggest we pray about it." Falling to their knees, bowing their heads and holding each other's hand, they prayed for guidance. Upon completing their prayers, Bethany began to observe the actions of the other contestants, which were quite comical. The Octopus was walking around the crowd, almost in a daze. Then with one hand he grabbed his own hair and pulled it hard. Next, he pounded the side of his head with the palm of his hand, apparently believing that this ritual would help him think of a solution. The Human Sponge turned over one of the barrels and sat down beside it, placing his elbows on his knees and covering his ears with both hands. He then began to rattle off names out loud, creating a trance-like state to drown out the noise of the crowd. It was clear that these two contestants were having trouble focusing on the problem. Finally, there was The Eliminator: He looked straight at Bethany and smiled, confidently believing that his pure genius would cause him to figure out the solution. He next took two of the barrels and placed them side-by-side with a third barrel on top of the other two. Climbing up on top of the barrels and organizing his hands and legs in what appeared to be a quasi-yoga position, he began to overlook the activities of the other contestants. Finally, he calmly closed his eyes, grinning as his dazzling mind contemplated the perfect solution to the problem at hand.

At first Bethany was mesmerized by The Eliminator's haughty confidence. Then she got mad. "Gabriel, look at that … that … big jerk! He thinks he's got this contest won just because I'm a kid. Well, he ain't seen nothing yet!" Bethany said, raising her voice in hopes that The Eliminator could hear her.

Gabriel responded with a smile, "What we do, Kemosabe? Tonto will help Lone Ranger."

"Gabriel, cut that out! Get serious, now. We're going to win this contest! We're going to get that Brahma bull through the barrel!"

As Bethany crossed her arms and began to think deeply, the clowns began to divide the coliseum floor into four sections by the use of large, lightweight dividers so one contestant could not see what the other contestants were doing. Then four colossal bulls were brought into the arena – one for each contestant. Time was marching on. Suddenly Bethany had an idea. "Gabriel, the note doesn't say we have to use these barrels here, does it?"

"No. It just says 'Put bull through barrel.'"

Bethany smiled, "Gabriel, I think I'm onto something. Follow me. I've got to hurry and get some help." Bethany told Oba to "stay" until they returned. She and Gabriel then went into the crowd at the stadium and asked twelve strong men to follow her. Just before she entered the coliseum earlier, she had noticed a round, wooden water tower elevated about fifteen feet above the ground. She figured that the wooden container was probably at least eight feet wide. She thought that, if the water could be emptied and the top and bottom knocked out, a bull could fit through it. Of course, it would take some fast action to get all this done and return with the hollowed-out barrel, but it was worth a try. Under Bethany's direction, they got to work. When she, Gabriel and the men returned rolling in the huge barrel, the entire crowd came to their feet as a deafening roar washed over the arena.

The other contestants knew something was happening, but could not see anything because of the partitions. The Eliminator was still in his yoga position and was amazed when the crowd's applause suggested that Bethany might be developing a solution.

Bethany had the men place the barrel squarely in the middle of her area. Next she called on Oba – the most athletic dog in the world, she was convinced – to help her with her objective. Placing her red bandanna around Oba's neck, Bethany whispered something in Oba's ear, and then said, "Go get 'em boy!" Oba was off like a bullet doing what he liked to do best – running and jumping! Oba headed straight toward the bull and, leaping high into the air, he bounded off the side of the bull as if to say, "Let's play tag. You're it!" The two thousand pound beast was puzzled at first by the dog's action, but became agitated as the dog bounded into the bull's broadside over and over again. The spectators were going wild as they began to yell in unison – "O-ba! O-ba! O-ba!"

Obadiah became more and more hyperactive as the crowd continued the chant. He ran to the very edge of the partition, turned, and with a full head of steam, careened toward the bull in a reckless fashion and leaped onto his broad shoulders. The bull stood frozen for a moment and then turned and kicked violently to remove Oba from his backside. Next Oba circled the bull seven times before finally running between his mammoth legs. Oba then lined up straight in front of him, eye to eye, no more than three feet from the animal's huge head and horns. The bull could take no more and began to snort and move one of its hooves in a pawing fashion into the ground. Finally, Oba did the unthinkable. Facing the bull, he got on his hind legs and did his "walk like Gabriel" routine, falling on his side only a foot from the bull's face.

Bethany could tell that the powerful animal was ready to charge, so she yelled, "Oba, watch out! He's coming after you!" Fearing for Oba's safety, Bethany took her replica rod of Moses, ran toward the bull's backside and wacked it to distract his attention so that Oba could escape. Jumping up quickly, Oba began to run, as the bull, distracted only momentarily, followed after him. The little red bandanna Oba wore around his neck only excited the bull more. As the full charge was under way, Oba steered the bull around the arena and finally toward the large barrel, running through it at full speed with the bull in hot pursuit. Bethany had run to the other end of the barrel, where she was holding over her rod of Moses a large red robe that she had borrowed from a woman in the crowd. This only infuriated the bull further. At the end of the barrel, the bull could see nothing but red as he continued to charge with rage in his eyes. Finally, the crowd went into pure bedlam, cheering at the top of their lungs, at the sight of the bull passing through the barrel following Oba closely. Bethany, like a true matador held her position to the last second and waved her red cape extended over the rod as the bull went flying past her.

The Eliminator couldn't stand not knowing what was happening in Bethany's partitioned area so he stacked another barrel on top of his roost to add height. He was in the process of trying to peer over the top of the divider when suddenly the uncontrolled bull burst through the partition and squarely hit the stacked barrels on which The Eliminator sat – hurling him almost twenty feet into the air.

Bethany grinned from ear to ear, as she said to Gabriel, "If this were team bowling, I'd say we've got a strike!"

Gabriel was overjoyed at her accomplishment and closed his eyes in thankful prayer.

As the crowd cheered, Bethany, placing Oba on her shoulder, waved her arms in the air and circled the arena as the whole multitude began to throw thousands of flowers to her in congratulations.

A single voice called out from the crowd. "She cheated! It's illegal what she did! She left the arena and used others to assist her in the contest! She must be disqualified!" As the crowd turned to find Bethany's accuser, they discovered that the voice belonged to none other than The Eliminator! He was determined that he was *not* going to lose this contest.

The horde in the arena began to boo and hiss at The Eliminator. Nonetheless, the head judge said, "We will consider this protest carefully. In the meantime, I am asking each of the contestants to write their response to the question, 'what have you learned?' and be ready to turn it into the judges' table when your name is called. You have approximately ten minutes to prepare your answer."

As he dusted himself off from his fall, The Eliminator grinned – a large, smug, confident, sickening grin – as he looked directly at Bethany and Gabriel. He knew that if the bull contest was thrown out, a good written answer on what he had learned would be all it would take to win the contest. As a college professor, his writing skills were excellent: He was confident that no one, especially not a child, could match his skill in this area.

Bethany's heart sank, and she almost began to sob. "It's not fair; the rules didn't say we couldn't do what we did. And I don't have a chance on the written part!"

Gabriel put his arms around her as he tried to comfort her. Looking her in the eye, he said, "Bethany, don't you give up, not now, not ever! You can do it! You're The Mighty Mustard Seed! Now, think about your answer. And remember to keep it brief," he commented recalling the judges' instructions.

Wiping the moisture from her eyes and beginning to control her emotions, Bethany saw each of the contestants writing furiously about all the things they had learned. Bowing her head in reflection, she asked God for wisdom in her response.

The other contestants hurriedly continued to write and rewrite their one page answers, polishing them to perfection. Looking over at Bethany, The Eliminator was not surprised that she had not written down anything: He imagined that the stress of summarizing all she had learned was too much for her. Bethany continued to keep her eyes closed tightly in apparent contemplation. The head judge announced that the responses would be reviewed in the order of the contestant's age, oldest first — The Octopus, The Human Sponge, The Eliminator and, last of course, Bethany. Finally, the other three contestants, one by one as their names were called, turned in their papers for the judges' review.

Each judge made comments on each paper received and silently transferred the suggested grade to the head judge. After the first three papers had been reviewed and graded, it was Bethany's turn. The head judge spoke up, "Miss, you must hand in your answer."

Unexpectedly, her mind became clear and like a single laser of light cutting through all of life's extraneous parts, an intense vision appeared in her head. Although risky and bold, she announced to the judge, "My answer is brief. May I give it orally?"

After a moment of thought, the head judge said cautiously, "No, I believe the rules require that it be written." (The head judge was not going to give The Eliminator another ground for a protest.)

"But it is only three words."

A dead silence arose over the judges and contestants as the words *"three words"* sunk in. Slowly, a murmur arose as the audience in the coliseum began to pass the word, "Her answer is only three words – three words!" Even The Eliminator was taken aback at such a bold move and questioned whether it was possible to collapse her learning experience into such simplicity. He also wondered whether her experience had been much different from his own.

After a few more moments, the head judge responded, "Miss, I'm sorry, but you must answer in writing."

Bethany, for an unknown reason, counted to confirm the number of judges before writing down her words. At last, on the back of the paper, she wrote her three words. Then taking a deep breath and with her heart pumping hard, she did something that no one could believe. Turning for the crowd to see, she carefully tore the paper into twelve pieces! The crowd was in shock and anguish, believing their favorite contestant had destroyed any chance of winning! The judges just shook their heads, as the head judge asked, "What in creation's name are you doing, young lady?"

Bethany smiled while mixing up the pieces and then began to hand one to each of the judges. On each piece of torn paper was a different letter of the alphabet, except for

one which was an exclamation point! The letters were: j a t
y h e r o s h e !

"You now have my answer," Bethany said. "And I'll give
you a hint, the first word is five letters and next two are
three each, followed by an exclamation point!"

The head judge did not know how to reply. Bethany
had responded in writing as requested. Her answer was
there. If he now allowed her to give an oral answer, it would
be protested by The Eliminator, and the crowd would not
be pleased and might even riot. If the judge refused to
attempt to interpret the answer, the crowd would think that
these twelve outstanding angels were lazy or, maybe worse,
not intelligent enough to figure it out. The head judge
decided to have the other judges attempt to determine the
answer. The angels were initially not happy as they were
forced to communicate with each other and to huddle
closely and exchange their letters and thoughts. Next they
placed together different combination of letters to try and
solve the puzzle created by Bethany's handiwork. Soon they
were laughing aloud and working as a team, discovering
different combination of words that didn't quite work but
were sometimes quite interesting (and, yes, possibly even
humorous), nonetheless. The crowd seemed amused also to
watch these pompous angels began to pal around – sharing
their letters and ideas with each other and acting a bit like
children at play.

Bethany held Oba firmly, anticipating the judges'
comments on her answer. Oba buried his head on her
shoulder as if he could sense the tension of the moment.

Finally, after about ten minutes, the judges had the
answer and quietly studied the words and gave their scores
to the head judge. He reviewed the scores and then stood
up and cleared his throat before making the
announcement. "Based on a review of the answers, we have
decided that we have a winner to this contest regardless of
the outcome of the prior protest lodged by one of the

contestants. We are impressed with this year's Super Semi-Final Champion, who has brought clarity and creativity to the winning answer. The winner shows outstanding wisdom, insight and vision. We the judges will not soon forget this contest or the lesson that we learned this day. At this time it is my great pleasure to declare this year's victor – who is none other than – Bethany Anna Clarke, The Mighty Mustard Seed!!!!" The crowd shouted a deafening roar of approval, as The Eliminator threw down his cowboy hat in disgust and dropped to his knees in frustration at his loss. The Octopus and The Human Sponge came by to congratulate Bethany on her great competition.

Gabriel grabbed Bethany and Oba and twirled them both around, as Oba let out a howl of delight. Placing them back on the ground, he had to ask, "Bethany, what did you write down? What were the three words?" Not knowing what letters she handed the judges, and not hearing clearly her other clues, he said, "Was it 'Let Love Rule' or maybe 'God Gives Hope'? Those would have been good ones."

Suddenly, Bethany was surrounded by well wishers who hugged her in the merriment of the moment. As the final mass of her vocal fans stormed the field and lifted her and carried her away in triumphant celebration of her victory, Bethany yelled over her shoulder, "I'll have to tell you ... laa-terrrr!!"

*   *   *   *   *   *   *

After celebrating with the crowd for almost half an hour and thanking each of the men that had helped, Bethany was tapped on the shoulder. Turning around she was shocked to see a smiling female face that she recognized immediately. "Old Woman I Know, what are you doing here?" Bethany said as the two of them embraced each other. The old woman then held Bethany's two shoulders and looked her square in the eyes. "I couldn't be more proud of you. You have done well, young lady. Congratulations!"

"Thanks," Bethany responded and then realized that the old woman had said the word "congratulations." "Hey, what happened to your spooner-sylloquatia?"

"Oh that. That's a long story. Why don't you ask Gabriel? He's the one that put me up to it. It's very difficult to talk like that, you know."

Gabriel began to chuckle, "Bethany I know it sounds silly, but I wanted to mix things up, possibly make you look at things differently. So I asked her to talk that way." Anyway, I think it's time you know who this woman really is. Meet none other than Ruth."

"Ruth? You mean Ruth, Ruth? I mean the Bible Ruth?" Bethany said as her voice trembled with excitement. "You're King David's great grandmother?"

Ruth nodded as she smiled.

"Wow! This is so cool! Never in my wildest dreams did I ever think that I'd meet you. I'm really glad to meet you, Mrs. Ruth!"

"And I'm really glad to meet you, Miss Bethany Anna Clarke – The Mighty Mustard Seed. You did great! Good luck with the championship round!"

Gabriel hugged Ruth as if to say goodbye and announced to Bethany that it was time to go to their next destination. Standing by Gabriel's side, Bethany and Oba, along with Gabriel, were transported by the JOY device to Kadesh-barnea to catch a good night's sleep before getting to see Moses.

Chapter 20
Messed Up — Big Time!

Back at Kadesh-barnea, the sun was high overhead when Gabriel served lunch to Bethany. Bethany had slept well the night before, resting from her competition. In fact, she was so tired that she had completely slept through breakfast. While giving food to Oba, Bethany realized how attached she had become to him. Obadiah, panting in the hot sun, looked quite happy next to Bethany, as he nuzzled close to her, using her body to create a small amount of shade for himself.

Gabriel stood up, having finished his meal and shaded his eyes from the sun as he commented, "It's almost time to go see Moses."

As Bethany continued to munch on her grapes, she couldn't help but comment on how ungrateful the Israelites had been toward God after spying on their Promised Land. "I can't believe that the leaders of the tribes of Israel were such big sissies. I mean, didn't they realize that if God was on their side they were going to get the land? But to come back and give Moses such an awful report on how strong the people in Canaan were and to even suggest that they go back to Egypt, that's incredible after all God had done for them!"

"Yes, and now you know why they wandered in the wilderness for so long. As punishment, the Lord forbade them to go into the land until forty years had passed, one year for each day the spies had been in Canaan. Only Joshua from the tribe of Ephraim and Caleb from the tribe of Judah were outspoken in their desire to take the land that God had promised them. They said to the people in Numbers 14:7-9:

> ... The land, that we went through as spies is an exceedingly good land. If the Lord is pleased with us, he will bring us into this land and give it to us, a land that flows with milk and honey. Only, do not rebel against the Lord; and do not fear the people of the land, for they are no more than bread for us; their protection is removed from them, and the Lord is with us; do not fear them.

"And it was a sign of which tribes would become the leaders of the Israelites that the tribe of Judah, which was David's tribe, and of the tribe of Ephraim, Joseph's son's tribe, would have men who proved to be the bravest," Gabriel said.

Bethany listened intensely as she patted Obadiah in her lap.

"Well, the time has come for you to see Moses," Gabriel went on. "Follow me over the next few hills." Bethany obeyed and, as she went to the far side of the third hill, she saw a great hoard of Israelites, with Moses speaking to the leaders who had just returned from their spy mission.

"There he is – Moses!" Bethany squealed as she saw him stand before his people, his arms raised to silence them. As Bethany and Gabriel approached, they could hear Moses speak.

"You have heard your fellow tribe leaders, but I implore you, do not make a decision to go back to Egypt without first hearing from Joshua and Caleb upon their return," said Moses, his voice quivering with emotion.

Another leader in the crowd yelled out, "Moses, they have been captured by the giants of Nephilim. They will not return. I say we depart this land for Egypt tomorrow at daybreak."

"Who are the giants of Nephilim? I don't remember seeing their tribe on your map," Bethany commented.

"Hush! I want to hear this. Something has gone wrong, terribly wrong! Joshua and Caleb must be in trouble," Gabriel remarked. As they listened, they overheard several men recounting the details of the two men's capture.

"Joshua and Caleb are probably dead by now, anyway," one man in the crowd interjected. "The men of Nephilim are huge. They make us look like grasshoppers. They could easily crush any Israelite with a single blow."

Moses sat down with a sullen look covering his face.

"In the name of Jesse, father of David, this can't be happening!" Gabriel cried out. "They're going back to Egypt! It's not supposed to happen like this!"

"Holy Moses!"

"You can say that again!" Gabriel commented. "This is serious stuff. In all my years of angeling, I've never, never run into a situation like this. If Joshua and Caleb don't show up, the whole history of the world could change. We're talking about an event that could affect three of the world's major religions: Judaism and Christianity, as well as Islam."

"You mean no Hanukkah or Christmas?" asked Bethany, looking uncertain.

"That's about the size of it. And possibly no Ramadan," referring to the Islamic holy day. Gabriel then folded his hands and raised them to his head, holding them there with a heavy heart.

"Can't you do something? I mean Joshua's got to fight the battle of Jericho and lead his people to the Promised Land. Why don't you contact God? He can straighten this whole thing out. Can't he? Are you OK? What's going on?" Bethany rattled.

"Please, be quiet, I'm praying. I'm trying to contact God. For some reason, I can't get through," Gabriel responded. As he prayed, he asked for forgiveness if history had been altered by his failure to keep the time travel device out of Bethany's hands. He also asked that he be given guidance to help free Joshua and Caleb and guide them back to Moses. Gabriel then, completing his prayer, lowered his hands and raised his head.

"Could we talk this over with Moses?" Bethany inquired.

"Well, we're in the past so he can't see us. Remember, only God can have us appear to people in the past. But I guess we could communicate with Moses. He would listen to me, of course, since I'm an angel. But what would I say? Angels are messengers of God, and I don't have a message. Plus, traditionally only archangels talk to Prophets."

"Gabriel, now is not the time for ... for ... protocol! We've got to do something!"

"You're right! I'm off to find God! But I want to check something out first. You stay here. Oh, in case you need one, here is a silent horse whistle if you wish to call a stallion from God's stables."

"Gabriel, a silent horse whistle? Now that's an oxymoron if I ever heard one!" Bethany blurted out, forgetting her situation momentarily. Before she could say another word, Gabriel was gone.

Bethany stood quietly for a few seconds trying to calm herself, despite her realization of the seriousness of the situation. "I ... I must not have a hyperspasm ... must stay calm," she whispered. "What to do? What to do?" she thought to herself as she closed her eyes to concentrate on trying to relax. As she waited, she reflected what she might do if Gabriel did not return shortly. Three hours passed in the hot sun without Gabriel's reappearance. Obadiah had found a spot of shade near a small bush and was resting quietly. Bethany finally decided that she could wait no longer. She must take action. She must find Joshua and Caleb herself, free them from the Nephilim and bring them here to Kadesh in time to stop the Israelites' return to Egypt. "I must find them, but how?" she spoke out loud in frustration. She began walking in a wide circle as she said to herself, "There must be a way to find out where they are." Just then her foot tripped over a small, black book that she recognized immediately as Gabriel's Bible. "He must have dropped it in his hurry to get away," she whispered. As she opened it, she saw one of the land maps that Gabriel had prepared for her studies.

"Now I've got it!" Bethany exclaimed, as she viewed the rumpled map. "All I have to do is read the part in Numbers about the spies going into Canaan, and it probably will tell me where the Nephilim live. Then I can look on Gabriel's map and find the exact location!" Bethany said excitedly as she began to review the chapters of Numbers closely. Finally, she stumbled onto the passage she was looking for, beginning at Numbers 13:32:

> So they brought to the Israelites an unfavorable report of the land that they had spied out, saying, "The land that we have gone through as spies is a land that devours its inhabitants; and all the people that we saw in it are of great size. And there we saw the Nephilim (the Anakites, who come from the Nephilim); and to ourselves we seemed

like grasshoppers, and so we seemed to them."

"So the Nephilim were the Anakites, but I still don't know where they live," Bethany mumbled to herself as she pushed her mind to use the macro-association powers that Gabriel had taught her. "Maybe I missed something. I'll go back and read the prior ten verses beginning with verse 22."

> They went up into the Negeb and came to Hebron; and Ahiman, Sheshai, and Talmai, the Anakites, were there... . And they came to the Wadi of Eshcol, and cut down from there a branch with a single cluster of grapes, and they carried it on a pole between two of them; they also brought some pomegranates and figs.... We came to the land to which you sent us; it flows with milk and honey, and this is its fruit. Yet the people who live in this land are strong, and the towns are fortified and very large; and besides, we saw the descendants of Anak there.

Bethany's eyes brightened as she said loudly, "They must be in Hebron with the Anakites!" Excitedly, she unfolded Gabriel's map to pinpoint Hebron's location. As she frantically reviewed the map, she began to hyperventilate realizing that Hebron was nowhere to be found. "How ... how could he," she said as she tried to calm herself, "how could he forget Hebron?" With map crumpled in hand, Bethany closed her eyes, being close to tears, raised her hands to the sky and said in a loud, forlorn voice, "Oh, Lord, help me find Hebron! All I have is this no-good map and a silly silent horse whistle," which she then half blew out of frustration. Falling to her knees, she began to sob profusely, feeling that the burdens of all the world were upon her shoulders. Obadiah, disturbed by her crying, came close to her and licked her hands and cheek, trying to comfort her. Suddenly, Bethany looked up and saw a cloud of dust appearing in the distance and moving closer toward her. As she rubbed her eyes to clear away the tears, she saw, approaching rapidly, the magnificent white stallion that had transported Gabriel and her to this place. Once the stallion arrived, he paced nervously as if awaiting her command.

"What do you know, this silent whistle does work," Bethany commented in a surprised voice. "But a lot of good a horse will do me unless I know the directions to Hebron." With this, the stallion stood on his bulging hind legs and moved his front hooves forward as he snorted wildly.

Bethany studied the horse for a moment. She knew that this was no ordinary horse, but could he understand her request? Finally, although she thought it a bit absurd, she asked the stallion, "Can you take me to Hebron?" The stallion snorted again as it appeared to nod its large head in the affirmative. Bethany then led the horse to a nearby rock outcropping so she could mount. She held Obadiah tightly in front of her, as she leaped on to the solid mass of muscle. Holding the stallion's mane with her free hand, Bethany's smile widened as she yelled, "Well, Oba, let's *Rock 'n' Roll!*" Like a gunshot, the stallion fired forward northward toward the mountain town of Hebron.

Chapter 21
The Disappearing Act

Bethany arrived in the city of Hebron about an hour before sunset. Hebron was indeed an important city during early Bible times. It was one of the oldest continually inhabited towns in Canaan. Located approximately twenty miles south of Jerusalem, Hebron was one of the highest points in the southern hill country of Judah – some 3,000 feet above sea level. Known throughout Canaan for its abundant water supply and substantial grape and olive production, Hebron was where David was anointed King prior to his moving Israel's capital to Jerusalem. It is easy to envision how Hebron and the nearby river valley of Eschol would look to desert travelers as the land of "milk and honey" promised by God in Exodus 3:8. Not surprisingly, it was a land desired by many and well fortified to keep intruders out and the Anakites or so-called Nephilim in possession.

When Bethany approached Hebron and saw the huge walls protecting the city, she wondered how she would ever get inside. Finding a low spot in the wall (approximately eight feet high) and believing that the powerful animal on which she rode could virtually fly, she gave the command

"Wall; Jump!" The stallion back stepped about a half-dozen yards or so and took off clearing the top of the wall by a good two feet. When she landed safely on the other side, Bethany hollered as she leaned to one side and patted the horse on its neck, "Boy! If my riding instructor, Ms. Kendall, could see me now!"

Quickly Bethany jumped to the ground, placing Obadiah gently at her feet, and surveyed the situation, as the white wonder of a stallion, having accomplished his mission, departed by easily bounding back over the wall. Bethany moved out from the alley where she found herself after the jump, with Oba tagging right behind her. Just ahead she saw a street full of carts filled with fruits native to the region. Standing nearby were dozens of merchants selling these goods to the people of the town. At first she was hesitant to go forward into the busy street, but then remembered that, according to Gabriel, she couldn't be seen, only heard. With this knowledge she began to walk among the local villagers, pondering the next step necessary to find Joshua and Caleb. Viewing the people as she walked, she thought that – while they were taller than the average Israelite of that time – they were no larger than most Americans. The Nephilim were certainly not giants, she concluded. Suddenly, out of the corner of her eye, she saw two young boys in their early teens, taking fruit from a cart and placing it underneath their robes while an old merchant some distance away was looking in the other direction. Bethany hesitated for only a second and then spoke up, "Stop that right now! Put that fruit back! You should be totally ashamed of yourself!"

The two lads froze in a semi-crouched position, as a few pieces of their "take" fell to the ground; they dared not pick them up, however, until they had located their accuser. The boys' eyes shifted from side to side and their heads tilted back and forth rapidly in a quite comical fashion,

Bethany thought, as they continued to scan for a body to go with the voice they had heard.

One boy whispered to the other, "What's going on? Did you hear that?"

"Where is she?" the other boy responded.

Bethany decided to teach the boys a lesson. "I am here, there and everywhere! I am a messenger and servant of God! Return that fruit at once!"

The boys hurriedly complied and then turned toward the direction of the voice without a body. Finally, seeing the little dog focusing on them curiously, they began to direct their responses to Obadiah, as if he were the source of the voice. "Are you truly a messenger of the great Baal, the weather god, the god of thunderstorms who brings life-giving rain so that we might grow our crops?" asked the shorter of the two boys. "We are honored to meet you. My name is Talmai, and this is my friend, Reiman." (Reiman was tall and slender while Talmai was much shorter and stocky in build.)

"I'm not a messenger of Baal," replied Bethany, not expecting this inquiry.

"Then which god are you a messenger for?" the other youth named Reiman probed.

She thought for a moment, her studies with Gabriel had not entirely prepared her for this inquiry. Finally, she blurted out, "Yahweh, Jehovah, the Lord of Lords, the King of Kings, Creator of Heaven and Earth, the one and only true God!" "There," she thought, "that should cover the bases."

The boys stood silently with puzzled looks on their faces, as they stared in wonderment at Obadiah.

Bethany placed one arm across her waist and with the forefinger of the other arm tapped her lips as she searched for another phrase. Finally it came to her, "I am a messenger for the God of the Israelites!"

Both boys' eyes grew wide, as one responded, "Oh, we have heard of such a god."

"Not such a god, THE ONE AND ONLY GOD!" Bethany said forcefully. "And you shall be punished severely for your sins. Yes, you will experience drought, pestilence and great swarms of locusts will eat your crops, and ..."

"Wait a minute," Talmai responded, looking directly at Obadiah who began to wag his tail and twist his head to one side, "we just took a few pieces of fruit."

"Yes, but the fruit was tainted!" Bethany yelled. (Or was it painted? She couldn't quite remember.)

"And we hadn't even heard of this god," Reiman added, "until the other day when the Israelites were captured." (Bethany's ears perked up.) "It's not fair."

"You have a point. God is most fair, but you have sinned in other ways, I imagine, by worshiping idols and other gods. I tell you what I'm willing to do. Do you know the way to the captured Israelites?"

"Yes," said Talmai.

"Well, I'll tell you what, Reiman and Talmai. If you will lead me to them and will learn to follow ten simple rules I will teach you, I will speak to God on your behalf," Bethany said, thinking that this was a fair exchange.

"Yes, yes! We will do it!" responded Talmai, staring directly at Oba.

Finally, Bethany realized that the boys thought the dog was communicating with them. "Why are you looking so strangely at my dog?" she asked.

"You are not a dog?" Reiman asked.

"Of course not. Obadiah is merely my assistant. Go meet the boys, Oba," she said as Obadiah moved toward the youths who began to pet him. "Oh, yes. One other thing," Bethany added, wanting to get another gripe off her chest, "you must tell the others here in this city that God is against human sacrifice. It displeases the Lord greatly. Got it?" (Bethany was thinking about changing their names to something like 'Isaiah' and 'Zephaniah' so that they would be more likely to remember their promise to follow God when one of the boys responded.)

"Oh, yes! We will tell them. But what shall we call this god? Who shall we say has sent us?" said Talmai.

Bethany recalled a similar inquiry by Moses after he received the Ten Commandments on Mount Sinai. She pulled out Gabriel's Bible that she had previously stuck between her belt and waist, and she flipped quickly through Exodus until she came to Chapter 3, beginning with verse 13:

> Then Moses said to God, "If I come to the Israelites and say to them, 'The God of your ancestors has sent me to you,' and they ask me, 'What is his name?' What shall I say to them?" God said to Moses, "I AM WHO I AM." He said further, "Thus you shall say to the Israelites, ' I AM has sent me to you.'"

Bethany, after reading the passage, said to the boys, "Tell them, 'HE IS WHO HE IS' and that 'HE IS' sent you."

"He is?" Reiman asked, looking perplexed.

"I mean I AM," Bethany said becoming somewhat confused herself.

"You are what?" Talmai piped in.

"I AM, I AM sent you!" Bethany responded.

"You are sending us where?" Reiman said, even more bewildered than before as to the meaning of Bethany's words.

"No! No! God is I AM."

"You are what?" Reiman repeated Talmai's inquiry.

"I'm not I AM!" Bethany said with some irritation.

"Listen, make up your mind." Talmai said. "Either you are or you aren't. But who sent you?"

"He Is."

"He is what?" Reiman began again.

"He is I AM!" Bethany said, trying to control her anger.

Both boys scratched their heads as they tried to decipher what appeared to them to be pure gibberish. One boy, Talmai, believing her language must be a riddle, decided to continue. "OK. Let's assume you're not, you are. Does that make you not, I am?"

"Yes. I think so."

"OK," Talmai continued, "If you're not, you are and you're not, I am, then I must be, I am. Right?"

"No. You're certainly not I AM!" Bethany said, clenching her fists as she spoke.

Talmai responded, "But you just said you aren't!"

"Aren't what?" said Bethany.

"You're not and that I am," Talmai said, placing his hands to his head as he tried to keep her comments straight.

"No! God is I AM and HE IS!"

"Is what?"

"HE IS is God!" Bethany yelled.

"We know he's your god, but what do we call him?!!" Reiman chimed in, sharing Talmai's total frustration.

Bethany could see she was getting nowhere. Then it struck Bethany square in the face: She was playing God's messenger in history without his permission! She must tread very carefully. Silently, she folded her hands and quietly mumbled to herself with a prayerful voice, "God, forgive me, there is much I do not understand. Help me. Help me to remember my mission to find Joshua and Caleb and return them to Kadesh, Amen." After a brief pause in which she gained her composure, she said to the boys, "God will tell you what to say when the time comes. Now lead Obadiah and me to Joshua and Caleb."

In less than ten minutes, the boys and Bethany were standing across the street from a heavily guarded building.

At the front of the building stood two Nephilim sentries. The height of these two men made Bethany think that there were at least two men in Hebron who would be solid candidates to play professional basketball. "Releasing those Israelites may be more difficult than I first thought," Bethany said to herself under her breath. As she sat down on a small stool she had spotted moments before and began to ponder her situation, the boys asked her many questions about her "God" and religion. She told them about the Ten Commandments that Moses had received on Mt. Sinai and of the importance of her mission to free Joshua and Caleb.

After almost an hour of discussion, Bethany finally said to the two boys, "I'm going in. You guys stay here with Oba and wait for my instructions." Walking briskly past the guards who could not see her, Bethany found inside a multitude of idols placed at various focal points. She investigated the rooms on the main floor one by one and found nothing to suggest that the two Israelites had been there. Suddenly, she spotted a door leading to what appeared to be a raised basement and followed the steps down the narrow passageway. There were at least six cell-like compartments. "This is the place," she thought. The first compartment was empty as was the second. To her surprise, in viewing the third, there were three pacing lions that looked very hungry indeed, secured in their cell merely by a large wooden beam across the door. Then she hit the jackpot. Looking through a small, box-like hole in the fourth door that was secured by a complex lock system, she observed two men resting on mats laid upon the packed dirt floor. "Joshua, Caleb," she called out quietly and waited for their response.

The two men jumped up, ran to the cell door and took turns looking outside, but could see no one.

"I have come for you," she said.

The men jumped back from the door for they could

still see no one. "Is that you, Lord?" Joshua said, hoping that his prayers that God would come free them had been answered, although neither man had ever heard God speak before.

"God is a child?" Caleb could only ask, surprised beyond belief.

"Maybe children are closest to God's true likeness. Maybe that's why He is so fond of children!" Joshua said, trying to make the development make sense.

"But it sounds like a female child – a little girl!" responded Caleb. "Why didn't Moses tell us?"

"Maybe the Lord didn't think we were ready to accept it. I must tell you, I'm certainly having a hard time believing it now! God ... God, is that you?"

Bethany almost said "I AM WHO I AM," but stopped herself, realizing she had better stick to business. "I am only a messenger of God. I have been sent to deliver you from the hands of the Nephilim and to transport you back to Kadesh-barnea, where your tribes and the other Israelites await your return," she finally responded.

"Praise God!" Joshua exclaimed. "Our prayers have been answered. What shall we do to escape?" he asked.

"Good question," Bethany whispered to herself, since she really didn't have a clue as to how she was going to get them out of this mess. Nonetheless, she wasn't about to let the men know that God's messenger was driving without a road map, so to speak. "Err ... you will ... you will wait until after dark. Then the plan will be revealed to you," she said, buying time to figure out her next move and possibly communicate with Gabriel or, better yet, with God, who could clear this whole mess up in a jiffy. Bethany sat down outside the cell and began to meditate on how she could free Joshua and Caleb and have them back at camp before daybreak the next day, when the Israelites were scheduled to start back to Egypt. Minutes passed; before she knew it, almost an hour had flown by. Yet she still had no idea, no "game plan" for pulling off the escape. She began to pace back and forth, mumbling and shaking her head as she walked and watched the sun begin to set through a small window at the end of the hall. "It's not coming to me. It's not coming. God, why aren't you answering? I need some help here! At least send Gabriel. I really, really need some help!" she said raising her voice as she began to weep, ever so quietly, trying to keep the men from hearing her cries for help.

Suddenly, one of the guards appeared at the other end of the hall lighting the torch lamps throughout the hallway. Although she could not be seen, Bethany, out of instinct, jumped behind a stone pillar. In a moment, the guard was gone. Bethany sat down again and with her sleeve dried her eyes. She felt like the assistant basketball coach at a major university with her team down by eight points and thirty seconds left in the game. Maybe "Super Coach" could pull it off, but what if she left the game to answer an emergency telephone call or, worse yet, was ejected from the game by a rookie official? Would her assistant be sweating bullets? "Coronary City!" she thought. As Bethany considered her situation, she turned to her side to see if anyone was approaching the long hallway. At the same moment, her Bible fell from her waist. Picking it up, she saw it had opened to a Psalm of David. For some reason, her eyes became fixed on Psalm 31, which she began to read quietly to herself beginning with verse 3.

> You are indeed my rock and my fortress;
>   for your name's sake lead me and guide me,
> take me out of the net that is hidden for me,
>   for you are my refuge.
> Into your hand I commit my spirit;
>   you have redeemed me, O Lord, faithful God.

Bethany then read on to Psalm 34, beginning with verse 4:

> I sought the Lord, and he answered me, and delivered me from all my fears. Look to him, and be radiant; so your faces shall never be ashamed. This poor soul cried, and was heard by the Lord, and was saved from every trouble.

After studying David's words, she thought of what situations he must have faced both before and during his reign as King of the Israelites. She read more and more of David's Psalms finding comfort and assurances in his words, until finally she read Psalm 37, beginning with verse 7:

> Be still before the Lord, and
>   wait patiently for him;
> do not fret over those who
>   prosper in their way,
> over those who carry out evil
>   devices!
>
> Refrain from anger, and forsake
>   wrath.
> Do not fret – it leads only to evil.
> For the wicked shall be cut off,
>   but those who wait for the
>   Lord shall inherit the land.

After reading these words, Bethany whispered softly, "God please forgive me for taking the JOY device without permission and, well, possibly changing history. Please don't blame Gabriel for my actions. He's been a great teacher to me, and I'm sorry that I've let both of you down. Please, give me wisdom and the opportunity to help correct this mistake. Oh, and also God, if for some reason I don't get back home, would you make sure my mom and dad know how much I love them. I mean I'm really sorry we had that fight. And I really didn't mean what I said to my uncle. He's a pretty good guy. He's real smart, and I think he really loves me. Please help him to forgive me for what I said to him. Amen." After finishing her prayer, Bethany said to herself, "I must be patient. God will show me the way in his own time." With that comfort, she continued to read the beautiful Psalms, for they soothed her troubled spirit.

Bethany finally fell asleep reading, with the "good book" in her hands. Just after midnight she awoke, stretched her arms and, as she yawned, said inexplicably the name "Daniel," out loud. Still rubbing her eyes, she wondered why she had said this and suddenly her simple binary association made her sit up and say "Daniel and the lions' den. That's it! That's the answer!" she almost yelled, as the whole plan developed before her eyes.

She had spoken so loudly that she had awakened Joshua and Caleb. As Joshua came to peer out the small opening in his prison cell, he said, "What's the answer? And who, in the name of Abraham, is Daniel?"

"Never mind Daniel," Bethany responded, knowing that time was running out. Scanning the cell area of the Israelites, Bethany noticed several large, old, canvas-type bags on the floor, probably used for carrying large amounts of grain to the storage area at one end of the hall. She quickly grabbed the bags and handed them to Joshua through the small opening in his cell door. "Here's the plan. We've got to make you guys invisible so those guards will think you have escaped and open your cell to see what happened. So get in these bags in the corner of the room. We also need for it to be very dark in here. What I'm going to do is to first bring you all the lighted torches in this dungeon hallway and have you pass them through your cell window to my friends, Talmai and Reiman. They will be outside waiting on the relay." Finishing her instructions to the two men, she said, "I'll be back shortly. Remember, be ready when I give the sign."

Bethany ran out of the temple, past the Nephilim guards, who could only hear a slight noise as she rushed by, but could see nothing. In a few minutes, she found her two new friends, along with Obadiah, sleeping in front of the building where she had left them earlier that day. Quickly, she awakened them and explained what they must do to assist in the plan of escape. Her final words to the boys were, "Don't be late; be there in ten minutes sharp!" Bethany then walked a short distance away and stopped to kneel and pray silently without interruption, for she knew the importance of her mission. In closing her prayer she said, "Dear God, I just want you to know that I have learned a lot on this trip out here to your land. I know I have made a lot of mistakes in trying to help Gabriel with this situation, but, if it be your will, help me do this the right way. Thanks God, I feel much better now."

Finishing her prayer, Bethany gathered herself and rushed past the guards. She bounded up the temple steps and back down the stairs inside that led to the cell area. She began to collect the lighted torch lamps throughout the hallway and then handed them to the two Israelites through their cell window opening. Joshua and Caleb, in turn, handed them out the back cell window to Reiman who was standing on Talmai's shoulders waiting for the relay. Then Joshua and Caleb placed the large sacks over their bodies. The sacks were in the most inconspicuous corner of the room and blended quite nicely with the beige colors of the walls. Finally, the men sat silently in the bags and waited as Bethany had instructed. Then the game began.

Bethany and Obadiah went to the front of the temple, where the two large Nephilim guards stood quietly. Suddenly, Bethany, facing the two men, blurted out, "The

Lord, Jehovah, God of the Israelites has freed your prisoners, Joshua and Caleb! You need not look for them, for they are gone!"

The guards shook their heads, rubbed their eyes and looked at each other in disbelief. One guard finally said to the other, "Where does this voice come from?"

"It comes from a messenger of the ONE AND ONLY GOD, the true God," Bethany responded quickly.

"It is the voice of a child," said the other guard. "Could such be a messenger of a god? Are we to be afraid of a child's voice? It is a trick! Our gods would *not* send a child to deliver their messages!"

"Your gods are false! There is only one true God! The God of the Israelites, King of Kings, Lord of Lords! And the Almighty speaks through the Prophets of Israel and through children messengers like me. And let this be a warning to you and your people, the Lord God has seen your wicked ways, your idol worship, your human sacrifices and finds it … uhh …" Bethany couldn't find the word she was looking for, so she blurted out, "just awful!" Then Bethany continued, "In punishment, he has given your land to the Israelites. Your only hope is to repent and serve them and their Lord."

One of the men laughed. "I will not fear the voice of a child – a child cannot harm me!" he said, as he looked around the pillars of the temple to see if he could uncover the body that must go with the voice. "The Israelites are locked up and could not have escaped. We have been on guard all night," the guard went on.

"It is too late. They are gone," Bethany said with confidence.

"We'll see about that!" said the other Nephilim guard, as they both turned and walked into the temple and down the back steps to the cell area. The steps were pitch black without the torches, and the men stumbled most of the way down the passageway. "In the name of our god of thunder, what happened to our light?" one guard asked.

Bethany walking along behind them responded, "The Lord God is the light of the world! He gives light and takes it away!" "Hey," Bethany thought to herself, "I'm getting pretty good at this. Maybe I should have my own TV show!" Suddenly, Bethany tripped and did a twisting, half gainer down the steps. As she got to her feet and dusted herself off, she looked up and said, "Just kidding, Lord."

As they reached the cell of Joshua and Caleb, the guards took several minutes trying to open in the dark the complicated locking system of the door to the cell. Both guards yelled to the men inside to answer, but all remained quiet. When the door was finally flung open by the guards, Reiman and Talmai, who were just outside the prison walls near the outside window, began to bellow a chorus of "Joyful, Joyful, We Adore Thee," which they had learned from Bethany earlier:

"Joy-ful, joy-ful we adore thee, God of glo-ry, Lord of Love; Hearts un-fold like flowers before thee, Open-ing to the sun above. Melt the clouds of sin and sad-ness; Drive the dark of doubt a-way; Giv-er of im-mor-tal glad-ness, Fill us with the light of day!"

(Bethany initially had them practice "Onward Christian Soldiers" but changed the song when she realized that it was a bit too premature, under the circumstances.) As Reiman and Talmai repeated the chorus, it was as if scores of child angels joined in to create a glorious noise to God Almighty. The guards stood speechless since they could not see the prisoners anywhere in the cell and the powerful song of apparent angels confused them further. (Even Bethany was taken aback by the chorus of voices outside.) As the guards stood frozen with confusion,

Bethany picked up Obadiah and walked over to the cell's rear window. As she stuck her hand through the bars and pulled in one of the torch lamps that previously had been handed to the youths by Joshua and Caleb, she gently placed Obadiah on her opposite shoulder. As the chorus of voices continued to sing "Giv-er of im-mor-tal glad-ness, Fill us with the light of day," Bethany proceeded to march around the cell twirling the torch as she would a large baton. The awestruck Nephilim men watched the torch light and a growling dog appear to magically twirl and float before them around the cell.

One of the guards uttered to the other, "I have never seen a god make a dog float in the air!"

Then Bethany said, as the singing continued, "Even the great Pharaoh of Egypt could not hold the Israelites when God wished them to leave. How could you, Nephilim, expect to hold these men prisoners against the Lord's wishes? Go! Tell your people to repent and give themselves over to the Israelites or they will be destroyed – for THE ONE AND ONLY GOD has promised them this land!" Momentarily, the guards began to stumble back in retreat from the cell. As they turned to run out the cell door, Bethany launched stage two of her plan: the youths hearing their cue "THE ONE AND ONLY GOD" quickly moved two cells down and threw a torch lamp through the back window into the cell containing the three lions. The lions awoke with a fury and, while roaring loudly, bolted out the cell door that Bethany had conveniently left partially open moments before. Seeing the lions charging down the hall, the guards jointly let out a blood-curdling yell and scrambled up the steps with the lions close behind.

"Well done!" Bethany shouted out the window to Reiman and Talmai. As Bethany peeked out the cell window, she spotted at least three dozen youths looking in her direction. "So these were the voices of angels that I heard! They are your friends!" she said to the two boys.

"But what in the world are they doing up at this time of the night?"

"They are like us," Talmai replied. "They have no home and live in the streets. We sent word to them that you were a messenger of the ONE AND ONLY GOD and needed our help. So they came!"

Bethany smiled. "Tell them all that God will be pleased. I think a miracle of sorts has happened here today. Yes, God will be very pleased!" Hearing her words, the children began dancing in the street, with hands in the air, and giving each other "high-fives." "Boy!" Bethany said to Oba who was now in her arms. "No one back home is going to believe this. High-fives have been around for thousands of years. Who would have thought it?" Finally, she said to Reiman and Talmai, "Meet us at the designated place in ten minutes." Bethany then turned to Joshua and Caleb who were quickly out of their bags, and the three of them scurried out of the temple in a flash.

* * * * * * *

The boys had located five donkeys to carry their party to Kadesh-barnea which was many miles away. Looking up into the starlit sky and holding Obadiah close while the donkeys made their slow trek over the desert, Bethany gave thanks to God for the guidance she had received and prayed all would go smoothly from here on out. As they rode along, Joshua had to ask, "Oh, messenger of God do not be vexed, but how shall we be able to make it to our camp by daybreak on such slow animals as these?"

Bethany at once realized that Joshua was right; it would take a miracle for them to make it to camp before daybreak. She had no answer, so she responded, "With God, all things are possible." She then began to pray for some divine intervention. They pushed forward across the desert for almost an hour, and finally she remembered the silent horse whistle buried deep in one of her pockets. Thinking she had nothing to lose, she blew hard on the noiseless whistle.

In less than a minute, thundering hooves could be heard in the distance. Bethany's heart began to beat quickly with excitement. As five majestic horses arrived to join Bethany and her party of men, they stomped and snorted circling about showing their powerful bodies that were ready for action upon command. Bethany immediately recognized her old friend, the commanding white charger that had brought her to Hebron. Speaking directly to this stallion, Bethany said, "We must get to Kadesh-barnea by sunrise. Joshua and Caleb must be returned. Can you help us?" The powerful steed nodded, its neck muscles bulging in the partially moonlit night, as the horse gave out a spine-chilling whinny to confirm the assignment.

As each of the riders mounted their supercharged transportation, Joshua said to Caleb, "These are no ordinary horses. They are like none I have ever seen before."

Then Bethany yelled with a smile on her face, "Guys, hold on tight – these babies can really fly. So let's *Rock 'n' Roll!*" The horses rode hard and long until finally Bethany saw the sun rising in the east. Watching the stunning brilliance of the sun creeping over the desert hills, Bethany was awestruck by the natural beauty of God's world and realized how alive she felt and yet how small and insignificant she was in the grand order of things. She became concerned, however. Would they be too late? Had the Israelites already left the camp?

Upon observing the full rays of the sun, Caleb said, "Oh, messenger of God, forgive me but I fear so that we are too late. Cannot God give us a sign that all will be well?"

Bethany was dismayed but she could not let the men lose heart. "You must have faith," she answered. "God will provide when it's time."

*   *   *   *   *   *   *

Finally, dead tired from the long trip but not letting up on their intense pace, the horses approached the campsite. Everyone, even Reiman and Talmai, was anxious to see if somehow the miracle they had all been praying for had come about. Rounding the final bend on horseback and climbing up the hill that overlooked the camp, Bethany felt her stomach knot sensing her worst fear might have come about. At the top of the ridge, they viewed the sight below – only a few traces of campfires from the night before and a single, large tent. The Israelites had left! That was certain! Bethany's heart sank, as she moved down the hill with the others to see why the single tent remained.

Nearing the campsite, Joshua cried out in a mournful voice, "God, great God, why have you forsaken us?" As he said this, Moses appeared from the tabernacle tent where the Ark of the Covenant was kept – the portable temple of God, used by the Israelites during their years of wandering in the desert.

"They have all left," Moses responded sadly, as Joshua and Caleb approached. "My wife, Zipporah, and I tried to stop them. We told them you would return, but they would not listen. All we have now is the Ark of the Covenant. They have taken everything else."

Everyone looked despondent as Joshua and Caleb fell to their knees, with fear in their eyes, and began to pray with Moses at their side.

As the men prayed silently, Bethany, after walking a short distance away from the camp, sat on the ground and began to weep uncontrollably. "I failed! I failed!" she said between her sniffles. "What is to become of this world?!" she said in total frustration.

"It would be a better place for all, if there were more like you, Bethany," said a familiar voice.

Bethany couldn't believe her ears; it sounded like

Gabriel. As she turned around quickly, there he stood, legs spread firmly apart with his arms crossed and a special twinkle in his eyes. She ran toward him, as he opened his arms to embrace her and finally gave her a big hug.

"Oh, Gabriel, I'm so happy to see you! We are in terrible trouble. The Israelites are gone!" Bethany blurted out as quickly as she could.

"Calm down, young lady," Gabriel commented, and then pointed to the hill across the horizon. "Look, José, can you see?"

As Bethany's eyes searched across the valley where the camp lay, she began to notice a huge storm cloud not more than five miles away. At the same moment, four lions appeared at the crest of a nearby hill and began to roar, while Obadiah, from his distant vantage point, joined the chorus by attempting to howl in unison. In a few moments, the lions began to descend toward the campsite.

"Gabriel, what is going on!" Bethany asked, still confused but smiling ever so slightly, hoping that this was a sign that their prayers had been answered.

"I know what to tell Moses! Let's go!" Gabriel responded, with a look of confidence on his face.

Gabriel told Moses and the others of God's plan. The storm had stopped the Israelites in their tracks just several miles away. Gabriel then explained how the Ark of the Covenant was to be set on the front of one of the two abandoned chariots located nearby and that the four lions, which were now calmly sitting in the camp, were to be hitched to the chariots – two each. One of the chariots would carry the Ark, Talmai and Reiman. The other would carry Moses, Joshua and Caleb. Both chariots would go triumphantly into the area where the Israelites were being held hostage by the storm. The two boys were to take the Ark by special handles attached to it to a chariot, being careful not to touch the Ark itself, since doing so could cause injury or even death to a human. Holding the Ark steady, the boys would stand in the chariot while the huge lions pulled it across the desert landscape. After Gabriel had finished his explanation, the chariots were prepared as specified and the men and boys took off toward the Israelites. Once the chariots began to pull away, Obadiah immediately ran and jumped inside the one containing the Ark and then bounded on top of it as if to act as a guardian of its valuable contents. It was quite a sight. Between Oba's howling and the lions' roaring, Bethany felt goose bumps of excitement. She almost yelled for Obadiah to come back, when Gabriel stopped her saying, "Let Oba go. He's doing the Lord's work, you need not worry about him."

After watching the chariot continue forward, Bethany inquired, "Gabriel, shouldn't we go with them?"

"No. Our job is done now. God and the others will take it from here. Watch!" he said, pointing to the clouds of dust being made by the chariots in the distance.

Bethany viewed the scene as the storm clouds seemed to announce the men's arrival with thunder that shook the countryside for miles around. Suddenly, as the chariots neared, the clouds divided and began to dissipate allowing the glorious sunshine to fall upon the Israelites. After watching for a few more minutes, Gabriel spoke up, "We must go. Stand next to me, Bethany." And in a moment, with a sudden flash of light, trailed by a band of superb blue butterflies, they were gone.

Chapter 22
A Final Prayer

It was Saturday night, one month and nine days since Bethany's accident. To her parents, it seemed like an eternity. Tomorrow was her birthday, possibly the last birthday they would ever spend with her on this earth. Mr. and Mrs. Clarke had faced the hard decision and had told Stopher and Genny about the seriousness of Bethany's condition, including the possibility that she would never regain consciousness and would die. The whole family had taken turns breaking down and crying uncontrollably during the night.

The next morning, as was the case every day since Bethany had been brought into the hospital, her Uncle Lot came by to visit. Most mornings he would have long talks with her mother and father about not only her condition but also about her life. He wanted to know all about her friends, her activities, her desires, her loves and her dreams for the future. Lot commented on several occasions that he was amazed at her sports' talents, and that she was so focused on college at such an early age. This morning he was especially excited as he began, "Nancy, I've got a little surprise for Bethany. It being her birthday and all, I'm getting something for her that she's always wanted. I think it will make her very happy. It's real cuddly. Unfortunately, it won't be available for another week. But, I wanted to do something special for her today – on her birthday. I hope you don't mind."

Mrs. Clarke was surprised but tried not to show it. Lot had never done anything for her children's birthdays before, although she had always invited him to their parties. "Lot, I – I think that would be very nice. What did you have in mind?"

"Well, this hospital room is pretty dull. I was thinking a party with decorations and hats, and we could sing 'happy birthday' to her and, well, maybe it would raise all our spirits a bit. And, you know, maybe Bethany might … I mean, I don't know – maybe she might hear us and respond in some way."

Nancy could tell her brother's intentions were heartfelt and was touched by his offer. "Lot, I think that would be nice. I'll go get some decorations later today."

"Well, Sis, if you wouldn't mind, I've got some in the hall that I thought we could use."

Nancy hesitated for a moment and then said, "Well sure, Lot, bring them in, and we'll take a look at them."

Lot stepped out and, when he returned, his arms were full of decorations – "cookie" decorations of every size and description: banners covered with chocolate chip, peanut butter and oatmeal cookies; streamers with ginger snaps, butter thins and cinnamon stars; napkins, plates, and cups covered with sugar, pinwheel and orange marmalade cookies – even the horns and hats were covered with various types of cookie decorations, including molasses, datenut, and chocolate macaroon cookies. Uncle Lot beamed as he placed next to the bed an enormous tray full of twenty-one varieties of cookies made fresh by his own hands only a few hours before. "I know we can't eat them all, but I thought we could wrap some up in my cookie paper and hand them out to some of the patients and staff here. Maybe it would brighten their day."

Nancy and Bob were surprised and delighted with Lot's enthusiasm for this special party. They spent the next thirty minutes with Lot, Stopher and Genny decorating the room and preparing for the delivery of the huge pile of cookies he had brought. Stopher and Genny couldn't believe how much fun their uncle was having while he worked with them to get just the right "look" for the decorations. Once the task was complete, Lot asked if he could be alone with Bethany. Upon the family's departure, the crusty old uncle sat by Bethany's bedside, holding her hand and began to whisper something into her ear. After a few moments of complete silence, he closed his eyes and wept silently. In order to regain his composure, Lot walked outside the room and announced that he was leaving for a moment but would be right back.

A few minutes after her uncle left, Dr. Williams stopped by. "Hi, folks. Just happened to be in the neighborhood and thought I would drop in on my patient." Dr. Williams always seemed cheerful no matter what, yet today his smile was hiding a more serious mood.

"Good morning, Dr. Williams," Mr. Clarke responded. "Not much to report, except Nancy continues to hear Bethany whisper or something late at night."

"Tell me about Bethany's whispers," Dr. Williams said raising his eyebrows.

"Well, Doctor," Mrs. Clarke followed, "I know it may seem strange but three or four times during each of the last two nights, I've heard something coming from Bethany's lips. I mean, it's not even a good whisper, but I know they're words, names of people."

"What people might that be, Mrs. Clarke?" Dr. Williams asked with interest.

"Well, it sounds like she is saying 'Moses,' and the other name is 'Gabel' or 'Gabriel,' something like that."

"Interesting. Does she have friends with those names?" Dr. Williams inquired.

"Not that I can think of," Mrs. Clarke replied.

"It's probably the nickname for some old-time professional basketball player," Stopher interjected. "She's always talking about those guys and how interesting their nicknames were."

Dr. Williams smiled, "Is your sister a big basketball fan, Stopher?"

"Is she ever!" said Stopher. "She knows more stuff about basketball than anybody in our school. You know, just a few weeks ago she stumped Bobby Barton with a basketball trivia question, and he's supposed to know everything there is to know about basketball. Yeah, Bethany knows basketball! That's for sure!"

Suddenly, the room became quiet as everyone again realized the gravity of Bethany's situation. Then Dr. Williams asked Mr. and Mrs. Clarke to join him in the hall for a moment. Outside Bethany's room, Dr. Williams began, "I wanted to let both of you know that I am very concerned about Bethany's condition. She's lost more weight and her heartbeat has become quite irregular. I don't want to alarm you unnecessarily but things don't look good. The next twenty-four hours may be critical ..."

Before Dr. Williams had finished, Stopher and Genny came running out of the room. "Mom, I think Bethany's stopped breathing! Hurry!" Stopher said, gasping with excitement. Within moments, Bethany was being wheeled into an operating room. While she was still breathing, her pulse had dropped precipitously to the point that it was no more than a faint "bleep" on the monitor. As the doctors and nurses scurried around barking orders at one another and setting up the necessary equipment to deal with the crisis, Mr. and Mrs. Clarke stood terrified, almost frozen from the sight of their daughter's quickly deteriorating condition.

*   *   *   *   *   *   *

Bethany stood close to Gabriel, as they once again viewed the Promised Land from Mount Nebo – the same spot where Moses had viewed the land – from the land of Lot's son, Moab, the land of the Moabites. Watching as the sun set over the River Jordan and the Salt Sea, Bethany was enraptured by the beauty of the moment and was trying to picture what Moses must have thought as he viewed the land that he would never himself enter. "Gabriel," Bethany began, "it doesn't seem fair that Moses never got to go into the Promised Land."

"Yes, he died here at Mount Nebo and Deuteronomy 34:6 tells us that God buried Moses somewhere around here. But I agree with you, it does seem unfair – life is sometimes that – unfair. But I tell you this, as unfair as life on earth may seem to be, it is counter-balanced by the Lord's afterlife. That life is very fair, indeed. And even with all its imperfections, life on your planet is precious and should never be taken for granted. There is so much more to be learned … to be shared …to be done. You never know how long you have on this earth, and God wants some help while you're here. To those whom God has given much, much is required. Don't ever forget that, Bethany. Anyway, it's time. We must go."

"Great, where are we off to next?" Bethany asked.

"Home."

"Home? What do you mean home? What about the contest?"

"You must return before it's too late. Come, you'll see," Gabriel responded, as he took Bethany's hand and pulled her beside him, adjusting his JOY device in the process. With a "zap" Bethany and Gabriel found themselves in a hall of Northview Hospital.

"Come on, we must hurry," he continued, as he led her

to the operating room. Just before Gabriel began to open the door to the room, Bethany caught a glance of her parents walking slowly with their arms around each other at the far end of the hall. Her mother was crying.

"Don't go to your parents."

"Why not?"

"To them you're invisible, and there isn't time ... you've got to get back to your body!" He pointed to the operating room door.

"Wait a minute. I mean, what if I don't want to go back yet? I'm the only child contestant. I've got more to learn, but you can teach me. I know you can. I've learned a lot already. Haven't I, Gabriel?" Bethany responded, becoming torn emotionally by her situation. "I mean, I'm in the championship! Can't I hang around a few more days and finish the contest?"

"You could win. I know you could. No question about it! But you must go!" Gabriel's face began to show concern over Bethany's unwillingness to move quickly.

"Gabriel, I can beat those smarty pants adults, but I need some help! Look at the Olympic athletes. I mean, where would they have been without a good coach?" Grabbing Gabriel's arm, Bethany began to plead, "Gabriel, please don't leave me. You've got to help me with the stuff I need to know for the contest!"

"Bethany, you will learn it. You've got all your life to learn it. But, please, you must get inside there!" he said as he began to push her toward the door. "We've got to hurry!"

Realizing what was happening, Bethany grabbed an arm of a large, heavy bench just outside of the operating room and held on, yelling, "Not until you promise me that I will go back to the contest, and you will be my coach!"

"Bethany, that's quite impossible!" Gabriel said, huffing and puffing as he tried to get her to let go of the bench.

As she held on tightly and tried to kick Gabriel away,

she yelled, "You're an angel, remember, anything's possible!" A number of people close by began to turn around and listen to the voices coming from the hallway.

"Don't you know it's not nice to negotiate with an angel!!" Gabriel responded, becoming frustrated and concerned, as he continued to try to pull her toward the door. After a few more moments of struggling, Gabriel said, almost pleading, "Bethany, you must go in!"

"Not until you promise!" Bethany said adamantly.

Finally, Gabriel gave in, "OK. OK! I promise! I'll do what I can!"

"Great!" Bethany yelled as she let go of the bench. "Now give me a hug!"

Gabriel was a little embarrassed but, recalling he couldn't be seen and knowing he would miss her greatly, hugged her tightly as he said, "Remember Bethany, you've got a lot of support back home – sometimes from the least expected places. It might surprise you that your uncle is one of your biggest fans. Try and get to really know him. He might just grow on you. And remember, if you can be an instrument in opening a heart to God's love – well, that's pretty special!"

Bethany smiled. "All right. That's cool. Now I've got to tell you something, Gabriel," Bethany said. "About those Geeks I told you about. I mean, don't be mad, but I kind of made up that part about them being from Louisiana. Do you forgive me? I mean, I'm really sorry I told you that."

"Yes! Yes! Forget the Geeks! I forgive you!"

A strange, small breeze began to stir in the hospital hall near Bethany and Gabriel. Bethany commented, "Where's that breeze coming from?" Suddenly, it intensified rapidly into a wind that began to wail.

"That's no breeze, Bethany. That's your life force, and it is about to leave your body for good unless you get back to it!"

Bethany looked into Gabriel's eyes one last time as she

held tightly to his arms and spoke in a raised voice so that she could be heard above the howling wind, "Just one more thing, Gabriel. I need to tell you my answer in the contest – 'share the joy'– that was my answer. Share the joy!"

"Oh … Share the joy. OK. OK. Great! Thanks! That's wonderful! Now, please, you *must* get in there! This is your last chance! You must return to your body now!" With that, Gabriel shoved her through the doors, and Bethany went to lie with her body on the bed brought into the operating room. The strong wind subsided the moment that she and her body were one.

Inside the room the doctors and nurses continued to work furiously to stabilize her feeble condition. Then, what had been the doctor's greatest fear occurred: Bethany's heart stopped cold. Dr. Williams frantically began to pump on her chest in an attempt to revive her. A full minute went by without success as Dr. Williams had the others in the room prepare Bethany for electric shock treatment as a last ditch effort to revive her. Moments before the equipment was functional, one of the nurses touched Dr. Williams and then pointed to the monitor. Without explanation, Bethany's heart resumed its pumping activity and the monitor showed her pulse rising, rising within minutes to the point where she was no longer in immediate danger of death. Within five minutes, she had improved to the point that Dr. Williams had confidence that her condition had stabilized. Beads of sweat rolled down his face, as he left the room to announce to Bethany's parents that the latest emergency was over. As the doctor was about to give them the details, a nurse came running into the hall yelling, "Dr. Williams, please come quickly!"

Dr. Williams and Mr. and Mrs. Clarke briskly returned to the room, Bethany's head was twisting wildly as she yelled, "You've got to promise me, Gabriel! You've got to! I'm in the contest! I'm in the contest! Gabriel, promise me! Promise me!" Suddenly, Bethany's eyes opened and then roamed around the room. Spotting her parents, she began to smile as they came into clear focus.

As both parents rushed to her side, Mrs. Clarke broke down with tears of joy. "My precious child, you've come back to us," she said as she held Bethany's face in her hands and began kissing her forehead, and continued to do so, for what seemed to Bethany an eternity.

"Mom, watch out, you're neutrinosing me again," Bethany finally said weakly, and then began to break into a wide grin as she realized she had truly returned home and was surrounded by her family.

"Darling, whatever are you talking about?" Mrs. Clarke responded.

Rubbing her eyes, Bethany responded, "Oh, it's just a word that Gabriel and I made up."

Mrs. Clarke remembered that this was the name Bethany had repeated over and over throughout the nights. "Honey, who is Gabriel?"

"Gabriel is the angel who entered me in this contest. He took me to the Holy Land, and I met Moses and Joshua and Caleb and two young Nephilim," Bethany went on.

The room became silent. "Honey, you mean the angel Gabriel who gave messages to people in Bible times?" her mother asked, hoping for clarification.

"Oh, heavens no! As you probably don't know, there are nine orders of angels. I can name them for you, if you like." No one in the room spoke. "Anyway, that Gabriel was an archangel. This Gabriel is just a plain ole angel. But he is nice and very smart. He knows things about the Old Testament that would knock your socks off. You see, he believes in teaching by macro-association. It's really the best way to learn about the Bible. He taught me how to remember the books of the Old Testament by using silly association games and making up a poem. So you want to hear my poem? It's called 'Genny's Sis' for a take-off on Genesis. It goes like this …

Genny's Sis throws *Ex-o-dust*,
While *Levi* teaches not *to cuss;*
And *Numbers* gives us one plus three,
Which equals *Dude-or-Ron-or me.*

While Joshua Judges Ruth,
The trial t[w]o Samuel is reported;
And *t[w]o* the *King's Chronicles*
      to be recorded;
While on *Ezra's Knee (oh my! ah),*
Pretty *Esther* is supported.

Job thinks poetry's no laughing matter,
He opens *P[s]alms* to hear *Proverbs* chatter;
And sings *Ec-cles-i-as-tes* if you please;
Or if you think it nice,
A *Song of Solomon* will suffice.

"Actually," Bethany remarked, "it's easy to learn about the Old Testament if you just learn about the family. You know, the twelve tribes, and who was related by blood or marriage. I mean you wouldn't believe it, but David's great grandmother was a Moabite! So David wasn't even a full-blooded Hebrew! And, of course, that was important because it shows that the God of Abraham, Isaac and Jacob was for all people who believe and follow in the Lord's path. And I'll tell you another thing; there were some pretty important women in the Bible, too. I mean, take Deborah for example. She was the leader of the tribe of Ephraim – you know, Ephraim was one of Joseph's sons – and, anyway, Barak, a general from the tribe of Naphtali, wouldn't even go to war against the Canaanites unless Deborah went with him. Uncle Lot's not going to believe that! But it's true! Right there in the book of Judges. Wow! I mean Gabriel taught me so much so quickly – like how to keep Elijah and

Elisha straight. Just say: Ah-ha! You see, it's easy. Gabriel says we need to read the Bible more, and teach it to others so that it's interesting. Which it really is; I can tell you!"

The others in the room looked at her confused, as Mrs. Clarke reached for and patted Bethany's hand. "Bethany, honey, don't you think it's possible that maybe you learned this over the years in Sunday school, and maybe you just had a long dream that helped you put it all together?" Mrs. Clarke asked, hoping this would possibly explain Bethany's sudden outburst of knowledge.

"Mom, it's not a dream. You've got to believe me! It really happened! I was in this Bible contest, and Gabriel taught me and even took me to the Holy Land. I mean, I went to the Salt Sea, which is now called the Dead Sea, but when I was there, it was called the Salt Sea. And I went to the Temple just before the time that the Babylonians destroyed it. You know, the Babylonians took the Jews away for many years before they were allowed to return and rebuild the Temple." Bethany paused and looked around the room, as everyone – Dr. Williams, the nurses and her own family – stood dumbfounded by her strange story and her wealth of newly-acquired knowledge. "Stopher," Bethany continued, "you had the same teachers I had in Sunday school. Did you ever learn about the Nephilim? How about this one? Which tribe was Samson from? How about Joshua? What family was he from?"

"I don't remember learning any of that stuff, Mom," Stopher replied.

"Stopher, I … I mean, don't you think that maybe you just forgot a lot that you learned?" Mr. Clarke interjected.

Before Stopher could answer, a little ball of fur suddenly darted across the room and jumped up on Bethany's bed. Bethany yelled, "Obadiah! What are you doing here!"

Dr. Williams looked shocked. Turning to his head nurse, he said, "How on God's green earth did that animal get into this hospital?" As Dr. Williams approached Bethany's bed to remove the dog from the room, Obadiah began to growl and show his teeth. Dr. Williams pulled back and turned to Mr. Clarke and said, "Mr. Clarke, I'm sorry, but surely you know that we can't allow dogs in the hospital."

Mr. Clarke responded, "Doctor, I understand. But let me tell you, I've never seen that dog before in my life."

"But your daughter knows his name!"

"Well, of course I do!" Bethany yelled excitedly. "Oba, you're my proof!" she said as Oba licked her face with excitement.

"Bethany, how do you know this dog's name?" Mrs. Clarke inquired.

"Because I named him when Gabriel and I were in the Holy Land."

Dr. Williams threw up his hands in disbelief, as the nurses began to turn to each other and quietly whisper their amazement. Finally, he said, "This is getting wilder by the minute. All right Bethany, why in the world did you name him Obadiah?"

Bethany reflected for a moment. "Well, you see, it's kind of a long story. Gabriel and I were at the Salt Sea swimming and this little dog paddled up toward us."

"When was this, Bethany?" her dad asked.

"Oh, let me think. Gabriel made me this great chart of the Super Seven events in the Old Testament. I hope I can remember it. Let's see, it was about 1400 B.C., give or take a hundred years or so, during the time of Moses. And Gabriel said that this sweet little doggie reminded him of the Prophet Obadiah, and I thought Obadiah was a good name for him."

"How did you get there?" Dr. Williams asked, intrigued by Bethany's story.

"Oh, Gabriel has a *JOY* device. JOY stands for 'journey over yonder.' It's a miniature time-travel machine. You just set the knob, push a few buttons and it 'zaps' you to the place and time you want to be in seconds."

Upon hearing this, one of the nurses held her arm to her head as her knees buckled and she began to faint. Fortunately, several of the individuals next to her grabbed her before she hit the floor.

"It doesn't hurt or anything," Bethany continued. "Anyway, we were listening to Moses talk to the Israelites when we found out Joshua and Caleb got captured by the Nephilim in Hebron – except at the time I didn't know it was Hebron – and Gabriel was afraid that the Israelites would go back to Egypt. That wasn't supposed to happen historically so it was a little scary, and I had to go help free them. You know, I wouldn't have been able to do it, except Gabriel left me one of his silent horse whistles."

"Silent horse whistle?" Mr. Clarke asked in disbelief.

"I know that part sounds crazy. I didn't think it would work either. I even told Gabriel that it was an oxymoron if I ever heard one," Bethany said as she looked down and affectionately rubbed Oba's fur.

No one in the room spoke for almost a full minute. Finally, Dr. Williams asked Mr. and Mrs. Clarke to step outside with him. After they were in the hall, Dr. Williams started, "Mr. and Mrs. Clarke, would you consider Bethany an extremely religious child?"

Mr. Clarke spoke first, "Doctor, she is a pretty good child, and we go to church regularly, but I wouldn't label her extremely religious."

"Bob's right," Mrs. Clarke added, "she's always been curious about things, but … I mean … we don't really sit at home and read the Bible every day, although Bob and I have been reading it a lot more since this ordeal began."

"Well, I don't read it daily either … but I must tell you I may consider doing so myself. Oh, my medical background tells me there must be some logical explanation for all this, but it's really strange – even miraculous. Watch her closely for the next few months. Gee! Nephilim! What's a Nephilim? I've been going to church all my life and never heard of that one. I still can't understand how that little dog got in this hospital in the first place You know it's against regulations, but I'm going to let her hold that animal a while longer. Something tells me there's a set of higher laws here that we don't totally understand," Dr. Williams said, as he and Mr. and Mrs. Clarke entered the room once again.

Seeing her parents again, Bethany grinned from ear to ear. "Mom and Daddy, you two are the greatest. I told Gabriel all about you. And he taught me some really neat stuff. Hey, did you know that Gabriel means 'strong man of God'? Even some people who went to college don't know that." Obadiah snuggled closer to Bethany as she continued to talk. "And I met Ruth, and this old man with these keys helped me through these really cool gates." Her family stood by still not knowing what to say. "Doesn't anyone believe me? I've been to the Holy Land! I really have!" Bethany said with some frustration showing in her voice.

"I believe you, Bethany," her uncle said as he poked his head around the crowd of people in the room.

"Uncle Lot! You do? I mean, what are you doing here?"

Lot walked over and, to Bethany's surprise, held her hand as he continued. "Bethany, we need to talk."

"We do?"

"Yes, we do," he said as he patted her hand.

"About what?"

Lot smiled as he looked directly at Bethany's eyes and said, "You've got brown eyes, Bethany, glorious brown eyes. I'm so glad you're back. When I realized we might lose you, I thought about what a fool I've been. Focusing on things that have no importance whatsoever. For the first time in my life, I prayed – I mean *really* prayed. And my prayer has been answered. Bethany, I'm ashamed to say it, but I've been so self-centered that I actually didn't know anything about you. I couldn't even remember the color of your eyes. But that's changed, Bethany. I've changed. We're going to get to know each other really well young lady, along with the rest of your family. I'm going to make sure of that! And Stopher and Genny, that also goes for the two of you," he said, as he reached for the other two children to join him beside their sister.

"That could take a *lot* of time, Uncle Lot," Bethany said with a grin, as they both broke into laughter, and Bethany wrapped her arms around her uncle's neck.

Bethany's mother began to weep at the sight of her brother and her children closely bonding for the first time. Mr. Clarke held his wife in his arms and pondered the transformation that had occurred before their eyes. Even Doctor Williams and the nurses got a bit teary-eyed as they quietly left the room to give the family time to be together.

*　*　*　*　*　*　*

After a long conversation with her family, Bethany grew tired and was returned to her hospital room to rest alone. Stroking Oba's thick coat, Bethany's eyes began to droop, and her mind wandered as she relived portions of her great adventure. She felt different now … calm, although she didn't know why. She wondered if reuniting Caleb and Joshua was the completion of her third task or whether that task was yet to come. Then, out of the corner of her eye, she spotted, glowing in the window of the room, a large blue butterfly. She smiled, watching the butterfly slowly flap its wings as if to say hello and goodbye. After viewing the butterfly for a few more minutes, Bethany peacefully fell asleep, as the medication and trauma of her experience made her extremely tired. Oba observed the winged creature and began to pant heavily. He heard a quiet voice say to him, "Oba, time for our next mission. Come with me." Oba turned to Bethany one last time and softly licked her face as a farewell gesture. Jumping from the bed, Oba then leaped in the direction of the voice and, with a "zap," disappeared out of sight, trailed, of course, by dozens of exquisite blue butterflies that slowly vanished one by one.

Author's Note

It is only natural that once a book is completed, one reflects on the journey that has transpired in its accomplishment. My reflections center not so much on the writing of Bethany's adventures but on the many people who have touched my life in the process of its development into an idea and completed project. I think of my first Sunday school class over 17 years ago in Simsbury, Connecticut, which gave me my first glimpse of what fun the study of God's Word can be when filtered through the eyes of our young people. And in each class since then, I recall with fondness the abounding energy and ideas that have flowed from those fresh minds. Thank you kids, each and every one of you, for you most of all have allowed me to experiment and better understand how exciting the Word can be when placed in a new container.

Outside the classroom, my journey took me to old friends and new acquaintances for support and suggestions, too many to mention entirely, but a thank you to these especially: Val and John Del Terzo, Natalie Bates Dixon, Reverend Paul Gamber, Reverend Bob James, Susan Kleine, Kate Merrill, Bill Robertson, Myka Kennedy Stephens, Robert Stewart, Biff Wilson, and my special friend and assistant, Lynda Lounsbury.

Support of family was critical in my completion of this labor of love. My deepest gratitude goes out to my two daughters, Katherine and Elizabeth, and to my faithful Sunday school partner and wife extraordinaire, Mary Clare, who more than any other bore the brunt of my magnificent obsession of turning my idea into a book. Much thanks also to my brother, Reverend Phillip Kearse, for his thoughts and generous input. For constant encouragement and support, my utmost thanks to my sister, Lynne Nantz, who almost single-handedly has built my library of books on Bible history. And one family member who was crucial to making this book what I dreamed it would be is my nephew, Garrett Nantz. Through his diligent efforts, great insight and creative ideas, this book has grown exponentially as has our relationship with each other. Thanks, Garrett. Those late night brainstorming sessions were fun!

A final cadre of people deserves special recognition and thanks. Two pilot groups of young people were developed to test fly Bethany's adventures. A number of very good ideas came from these pilot groups. Thanks to the following young people at St. James United Methodist Church: Caitlin Baggett, Megan Gallagher, Ashton Lager, Alex Orr, Caroline Orr, Colin Shore, and Witt Weldon. Thanks also to those young people at Mt. Pisgah Christian School who gave me valuable feedback and insight.

Printed in the United States
35179LVS00002B/319-324

9 781594 675348